The Heritage of
The Kingdom of Saudi Arabia

End pages: *Interior court of Qasr al-Muraba. Built in 1935, the palace was King Abdulaziz's official residence when in Riyadh.*

The Heritage of The Kingdom of Saudi Arabia

WAHBI AL-HARIRI-RIFAI
MOKHLESS AL-HARIRI-RIFAI

THE HERITAGE OF THE KINGDOM OF SAUDI ARABIA
First published in 1990 by
GDG PUBLICATIONS
A division of The Georgetown Design Group, Inc.
1301 20th Street, N.W. Washington, D.C. 20036, U.S.A.

© GDG PUBLICATIONS, 1990

ALL RIGHTS RESERVED. No part of this publication may be reproduced, transmitted or used in any form or by any means—graphic, electronic, or mechanical, including photocopying, recording, taping, or any type of information storage and retrieval systems—without written permission from the publisher.

Library of Congress Cataloguing in Publication Data applied for.

ISBN 0-9624483-0-3

DESIGN: GDG Graphic & Advertising, Washington, D.C.
TYPESETTING: Hot Type Ltd., Washington, D.C.
COLOR SEPARATION: Pioneer Graphic Scanning, Malaysia
PRINTING: Eurasia Press, Singapore

AUTHORS' NOTES

This book is the result of over 15 years of travel in the Kingdom of Saudi Arabia, as well as the product of an endless cycle of research, review, and evaluation. While *The Heritage of the Kingdom of Saudi Arabia* represents the combined vision of two very close yet extremely different people, a father and a son, it is undeniably the product of the invaluable love and ongoing support of our families. The book is also the result of the efforts of numerous individuals.

Our appreciation goes to Muhammad al-Hamdan for his early assistance in delineating the scope of the book, and to Belkacem Baccouche for his scholarly review of the organizational and stylistic content of the manuscript.

Special thanks are owed to Imad el-Hajj for his assistance with the Arabic reference texts, and much appreciation goes to Ida Audeh and Zeina Azzam Seikaly for their help in reviewing and editing the manuscript.

Our heartfelt thanks are owed to Hamad Muhammad al-Abdali, Johara H. Alatas, and Frances Harper for lending us their expertise in reviewing a seemingly endless number of transparencies and for helping us with the critical task of identifying and editing the book photographs.

Our very special gratitude goes to Helen Khal for having reviewed the manuscript in its last stages and for having so generously contributed her talent to the forging of the final text.

The production of the book was greatly facilitated by the efficient coordination efforts of Jeanne K. Rose, the meticulous design assistance of Marya Mueller, and the most professional cooperation of Stewart S.S. Sum and Allan Fong.

TRANSLITERATION

The transliteration style adopted in this book was developed with special regard for readers who are not familiar with Arabic.

In an effort to avoid overburdening the text with symbols that would confuse the reader, the Arabic consonants *ayn* and *hamzah*, as well as diacritical marks that would distinguish between long and short vowels have been omitted

Also, the Arabic word for "son" was transliterated to conform with the Arabic spelling of *ibn* and *bin*. The scholarly abbreviation *b.* is not used as it would be unrecognizable by readers who are unfamiliar with Arabic.

Most Arabic names have been transliterated, except those names that have acquired a widely accepted form in the West, or a common transliteration in the Kingdom. A hyphenated *al* (al-) represents the Arabic definitive article, and a non-hyphenated *Al* indicates relation to a main family or dynasty.

THE HERITAGE OF THE KINGDOM OF SAUDI ARABIA

Contents

I. Introduction
His Royal Highness Prince Salman bin Abdulaz[iz]

II. Acknowledgments
Wahbi Al-Hariri-Rifai

III. Foreword
Mokhless Al-Hariri-Rifai

IV. Historical Overview

Ancient History
The Prehistoric Era
Tell Halaf
The Ubaid Civilization
The Dilmun Civilization

Pre-Islamic Arab Tribes
The Baeda Arabs
The Qahtani Arabs
The Ismaeli Arabs
The Quraysh Tribe

The Emergence and Spread of Isla[m]
The Prophet Muhammad
Islam and the Holy Quran
The Righteous-Caliphs
The Umayyads and the Transfer of the Caliph[ate to] Damascus
The Abbassids and the Transfer of the Caliph[ate to] Baghdad
The Ottoman Turks and the Transfer of the [Caliphate] to Constantinople

The Kingdom of Saudi Arabia
Shaikh Muhammad Abdulwahab's Call to Ref[orm]
The House of Saud
The Birth of The Kingdom of Saudi Arabia

V. Ancient Routes — 31

Ancient Trade and the Arabian Peninsula
- The Role of the Peninsula Before Islam
- Ancient Land Routes
- The Hajj Routes
- Caravans and Travel Stations
- European Trading Activities with the Orient
- The Hijaz Railroad Between Damascus and Madinah

Archaeological Research
- Western Travellers
- The Exploration of Arabia
- Drawings and Inscriptions

VI. Nature — 83

The Arabian Peninsula

The Kingdom of Saudi Arabia
- Al-Hasa
- Najd
- The Hijaz
- Tihamah
- Water Resources

VII. Architecture — 155

Architectural Overview
- Pre-Islamic Architecture
- Islamic Architecture

Architectural Types
- The Tent
- The Mosques
- Regional Architectural Types
- Ornamentation and Construction

VIII. Markets and Crafts — 249

Trade and the Arabian Peninsula
- Ancient Arabian States
- The Commercial Importance of Makkah and Madinah
- Seasonal Markets

Crafts
- Mines
- Metals
- Pearls and Precious Stones
- Textiles, Leather, and Fur
- Pottery
- Wood

IX. Bibliography — 307

INTRODUCTION

Inspired by the vision of its founder, King Abdulaziz Al Saud, and by the dedication of his sons, Kings Saud, Faisal, and Khalid, the Kingdom of Saudi Arabia has attained prominence in world affairs. Guided by the Custodian of the Two Holy Mosques, King Fahd bin Abdulaziz, the Kingdom has become a symbol of prosperity, stability, and respect for traditional values.

The Kingdom of the 1990s is a modern and technologically advanced nation dedicated to the well-being of its citizens and committed to providing special care and attention to the millions of pilgrims who, in ever increasing numbers, visit the holy cities of Makkah and Madinah annually.

As we reflect on the achievements of past decades and look ahead to the challenges of the next century, we have come to appreciate the important role that our unique heritage plays in shaping our future while preserving our Islamic beliefs and values.

At a time when the international community joins a new generation of Saudis in showing a genuine interest in the Kingdom's heritage, we are extremely pleased to have encouraged and sponsored the efforts that led to the publication of *The Heritage of the Kingdom of Saudi Arabia*. The book thoroughly explores the numerous facets of our beloved heritage and embodies the extensive effort of its authors, their heartfelt commitment, and their creative talent.

It is our hope that *The Heritage of the Kingdom of Saudi Arabia* will be widely appreciated, and that it will encourage other researchers, scholars, and artists to further explore and understand the Kingdom's roots and heritage.

Our sincere appreciation is extended to the authors for their remarkable achievement, and our full support and warmest encouragement accompany them as they begin their work on their next significant book, *The Spiritual Edifices of Islam*.

The Governor of Riyadh
Salman bin Abdulaziz

ACKNOWLEDGEMENTS

I am honored and privileged to have been able to work for so many years toward the completion of this book. From the outset, the invaluable patronage of the Custodian of the Two Holy Mosques, King Fahd bin Abdulaziz Al Saud, of Crown Prince Abdallah bin Abdulaziz, and of Second Deputy Prime Minister Prince Sultan bin Abdulaziz, has been a constant source of pride, encouragement, and inspiration.

I am specially grateful to His Royal Highness Prince Salman bin Abdulaziz, the governor of Riyadh. His trust in my efforts was unfailing, and his valuable support made my journeys throughout the Kingdom possible. Without his gracious and sustained endowment I would not have completed my work.

I must also express my heartfelt gratitude to His Royal Highness Prince Bandar bin Sultan, the Kingdom's ambassador to Washington. His esteemed interest in the book permitted its publication in a timely fashion.

I address my very special thanks to the Kingdom's officials in the various provinces, especially Riyadh, for their most courteous and kind cooperation. Their assistance, responsiveness and guidance were instrumental in helping me in my research.

Special recognition is also owed to Shaikh Misfer Suleiman al-Misfer for his invaluable encouragement, confidence and support.

Ever since I started working on the book, in 1969, I have benefited from the works of several scholars. In this regard, I must recognize the noted dean of Saudi historians, the late Shaikh Muhammad bin Blehed, and particularly his authoritative book *Sahih al-Akhbar*. I also wish to gratefully acknowledge the writings and deep insights of Shaikh Hamad al-Jasir, and I am specially indebted to Shaikh Abdallah bin Khamis who enlightened my research with his knowledge and wisdom.

Much appreciation is owed to Dr. Abdallah H. Masry, director of the Kingdom's Antiquities and Museums, for his valuable suggestions and encouragement. My gratitude also goes to Dr. Abdulrahman al-Ansari, chairman of the Department of Archaeology and

Museology at King Saud University, for the most significant information and scientific data he so kindly shared with me. Additionally, I am happy to recognize the advice and encouragement so generously provided by King Saud University's noted Islamic archaeologist, Dr. Saad bin Abdulaziz al-Rashid.

My sincere thanks are also extended to the numerous other scholars and researchers who, in the Kingdom and abroad, took a heartening interest in my work and demonstrated a genuine concern toward the preservation of the Kingdom's heritage.

I am also very indebted to the people of the Kingdom, for in the true tradition of the Arabian Peninsula they have always met me with their kind hospitality. During twenty years of travel and research they extended their friendship and provided me with the assistance I needed. Thanks to them, I was able to overcome the obstacles inherent to the completion of the task I had set for myself.

Finally, I wish to thank my family for their steadfast understanding, patience, and unyielding support.

May God turn my efforts into the good I had hoped to achieve. If I have fallen short of my goal I pray that someone else may complete what I have started and may succeed where I have failed.

Wahbi Al-Hariri-Rifai

Foreword

Since His Majesty King Abdulaziz Al Saud laid down the cornerstone of the Kingdom of Saudi Arabia, the country has made giant strides and attained an enviable standing among all nations.

In a relatively brief period of time, the sons of King Abdulaziz led the Kingdom into a quantum leap that has brought progress and prosperity to its most remote areas. Over the years, scholars, scientists, and artists the world over have witnessed and documented the advances and extraordinary development that have been achieved in all domains.

As a new generation comes of age, many vestiges of the past have fallen prey to the early stages of development. Fortunately, a relatively recent but thorough national effort is uncovering a wealth of archaeological and historical sites that were previously unrecorded or buried under the ever-shifting desert sand. As a result of the magnitude of the new discoveries, the citizens of the Kingdom have become increasingly aware, proud, and appreciative of their remarkable heritage.

With the passage of time and the acceleration of progress in all walks of life, it is hoped that the publication of *The Heritage of the Kingdom of Saudi Arabia* will contribute to a wider and true appreciation of the Kingdom's rich cultural legacy.

Mokhless Al-Hariri-Rifai

HISTORICAL OVERVIEW

Left: *Sunrise over the old desert route to Makkah, Najd.*
West of the city of Riyadh.
Following overleaf: *Sunrise over the historic site of al-Diriyah, Najd.*
West of the city of Riyadh.

Historical Overview

Ancient History

Until recently, very little was known about the early inhabitants of the Arabian Peninsula. Modern archaeological research and excavations have unveiled some of the mystery surrounding the prehistoric peoples of this area. As a result, it is now widely accepted that today's Arabian deserts were neither all desert nor completely uninhabited.

The discoveries support the belief that in prehistoric times the Peninsula was attached to East Africa. When most of Europe was still in the Ice Age, a more clement weather existed over the land expanse now known as the Arabian Peninsula.

Some of the fossil remains found northeast of Riyadh, near the historical site of Thaj, as well as in other locations, suggest that large mammals now extinct probably wandered from Africa to Arabia and Central Asia.

The Prehistoric Era

While the history of many regions in Africa, Arabia, Central Asia, and India has not yet been thoroughly researched, it is believed that 100,000 years ago a wave of Homo sapiens migrated out of eastern Africa. Some experts suggest that at the time, Arabia's now dry lakes and rivers had an abundance of water and offered a lush and welcoming environment for these Stone Age hunter-gatherers.

In their quest for survival, the early nomads used the escarpments' ubiquitous caves as shelter. Excavations conducted throughout the Peninsula have uncovered a wealth of Stone Age tools and illustrations. The diversity and richness of the flint axes, borers, knives, scrapers, and arrow heads found in al-Dawadmi, some 210 miles west of Riyadh, are equaled only by the abundant discoveries made in some of the most remote parts of the vast desert expanse known as the Empty Quarter (*Rub al-Khali*). The geographical spread of the discovered sites attests overwhelmingly to the long and well-established presence of the Peninsula's early inhabitants.

It is thought that some 15,000 years ago, a gradual but major weather change resulted in a worldwide warming trend. As a result, the Peninsula's streams dried up, the lakes vanished, and the forests shrank.

Faced with harsher living conditions, some of the early inhabitants migrated north while others settled in the pockets of remaining arable land or adopted a nomadic way of life. During the Neolithic period (8500-5000 B.C.) the new agro-based communities gave birth to sedentary village life. Sheep, goats, and cattle were domesticated and some early form of trade appears to have evolved around the exchange of certain items. Obsidian and sharp knife blades made from it, as well as precious stones such as agate, turquoise, and steatite, were prized items in the new barter economy.

Sedentary life also gave birth to numerous crafts, like weaving and pottery. Beginning around 6000 B.C., the development of pottery-making not only resulted in a change in diet, food preparation, and food preservation, but also introduced a new major trading commodity.

Despite the significant archaeological discoveries made during the last twenty years, it is still much too early to confirm with any certainty the chronological order of the rise and decline of civilizations in and around the Arabian Peninsula. Archaeological evidence does indicate, however, that in approximately 5000 B.C. a major socio-cultural change transformed the simple Neolithic life of some farming and fishing villages into the more organized societies of Tell Halaf, Ubaid, and Dilmun.

TELL HALAF

The civilization of Tell Halaf emerged on the Khabur River in northern Syria between 5000 and 4500 B.C. It was named after the Halaf hill located near the city of Ras al-Ain. The civilization, first discovered between 1911 and 1929, is thought to have developed in the ancient city of Gozan, whose inhabitants lived in agricultural settlements and excelled in pottery-making. Their beautifully painted pottery seems to have been exported to various parts of the region; samples of it have been unearthed in sites close to Lake Van in Turkey, 190 miles northeast of Tell Halaf, and in cities in Mesopotamia and the Arabian Gulf, up to 780 miles away.

THE UBAID CIVILIZATION

Various settlements that date back to 4500 B.C. existed in the northwestern parts of the Arabian Peninsula. They were part of the Ubaid civilization, named after Mount Ubaid (*Tell al-Ubaid*), where some of the early discoveries regarding this civilization were made between 1913 and 1914. Most of the settlements were located on the Arabian Gulf or in areas close to the coastal region known today as al-Hasa. More than thirty sites belonging to the Ubaid civilization were discovered on the western shore of the Gulf, four of which were settlements.

The Ubaid civilization represents the earliest known phase of the primitive era of eastern Arabia. The shapes and unique geometric patterns of Ubaid pottery are fashioned in colors ranging from red to brown to black. Similar pottery samples were excavated in a number of sites located in the proximity of several eastern oases, such as Ain Qannas and Dosariyah near Hofuf. Other samples were identified in several islands in the Arabian Gulf, even in distant Persian cities like Sussa and Persepolis. Related patterns also were found in Ugarit (*Ras Shamra*) near Latakia in northern Syria, about 800 miles away.

Excavations of Ubaid pottery in northern and southern Iraq provide further evidence that the Ubaid civilization had reached those areas. Samples were unearthed in Tell Hassunah and Nineveh in the north, and Ur, Lagash, and Hajj Muhammad in the south.

The discovery of Ubaid pottery was considered an important development because of its similarities in color, design, and artistic attributes to the pottery of Tell Halaf. Thus, it is believed that the Ubaid civilization must have preceded or coincided with that of Tell Halaf.

THE DILMUN CIVILIZATION

The Arabian Peninsula became the object of increased archaeological interest as a result of the discoveries of a Danish team sent by the Aarhus Museum in the 1950s. The team excavated various areas in Oman, Abu Dhabi, Qatar, Bahrain, and Kuwait. It discovered the city of Dilmun, Bahrain's ancient capital and the center of the civilization that prevailed in the Arabian Peninsula's eastern coast as early as 5000 B.C. and reached its zenith around 2000 B.C. Ancient Sumerian inscriptions, using the name Ni-Tukki for Dilmun, refer to it as an important hub on the trade routes to the Indian subcontinent. These findings indicate that Bahrain was a "paradise on earth" whose fertility and prosperity were praised in Sumerian legends.

Dilmun's presence extended inland and included al-Hasa, a major part of what is now Saudi Arabia's Eastern Province. Basing their view on the discovery of more than 100,000 burial mounds in Bahrain, archaeologists say that the ancient people of Dilmun may have lived on the mainland and used the island of Bahrain as a burial ground.

Dilmun, Magan, and Melukha are mentioned in Sumerian and Akkadian inscriptions dating back to 2360 B.C., when Akkad, the first known major city-state in world history, was established in Mesopotamia. Historians speculate that Magan, with its capital Bahla, was located in modern Oman. Melukha is thought to have been on the western coast of the Indian subcontinent, in the Sind region. The inscriptions indicate that Magan and Melukha had extensive trade relations with Dilmun.

It is important to note that the emergence of the first Mesopotamian cities appears to have coincided with the waning of the Ubaid civilization. Accordingly, historians believe that harsher climatic and living conditions encouraged successive waves of inhabitants of the Arabian Peninsula to migrate in large numbers to Mesopotamia, thus contributing to the development of the first settlements there. Those who remained in the southern parts of the Peninsula adapted to their environment and constituted the ancient Arab tribes.

PRE-ISLAMIC ARAB TRIBES

The Arab population of the Peninsula in ancient times is generally divided into three major Semitic tribes: the Baeda Arabs, the Qahtani Arabs, and the Ismaelites, or Adnani Arabs. Very little is known about the history of these tribes, especially the Baeda Arabs. Some of the available information has been conveyed by Egyptian, Persian, Roman, and Greek historians who lived around the same time and had some contact with the tribes. Other insights have been gleaned from early Arabic poetry. To be sure, modern archaeological research will yield a wealth of new information on the pre-Islamic Arab tribes.

THE BAEDA ARABS

The *Baeda,* or vanished tribes, are part of the Amalekites, a group that inhabited the Arabian Peninsula and Syria. The little information available about the Baeda Arabs refers to a series of conflicts and wars between them and other tribes, such as the people of Aad, who inhabited Hadramaut and Bahrain in approximately 1000 B.C.; the people of Thamud, who preceded the Nabateans in building stone houses around 586 B.C.; the tribes of Tasam and Jadis, who inhabited Najd around 500 B.C.; and the Nabateans, who inhabited Petra and Madain Saleh as early as 312 B.C.

THE QAHTANI ARABS

Named after Qahtan, one of their prominent ancestors, the Qahtani Arabs are believed to represent a case of reverse migration—from Mesopotamia to the southwestern region of the Arabian Peninsula. They settled in Yemen and gave rise to many famous dynasties such as the Mineans (1120-630 B.C.), Sabaeans (850-150 B.C.), Himayrites (290 A.D.), and Tababians (525 A.D.).

Aided by a mild climate and regular rains, the Qahtanis terraced the fertile slopes of their mountains and engaged widely in agriculture. Cities built on active trade routes, coupled with broad access to the sea, assured their prosperity in commerce; merchandise was unloaded in Qahtani harbors before being transported to other parts of the Peninsula. These Arab tribes also were known for their craftsmanship, particularly for tanning hide and making swords.

The Qahtanis built important cities like Sanaa and Marib, constructed irrigation networks, and made significant efforts to control their water resources. The famous Marib Dam, which they constructed during the eighth or ninth century B.C., survived until 543 A.D. despite its occasional flaws and the repairs it sustained over the centuries.

The destruction of the Marib Dam led many Yemeni tribes to migrate north to neighboring Arab lands. During this period, southern Arabia lost much of its importance, but the city of Makkah continued to flourish and three Arab dynasties rose to prominence: the Lakhmis, who prevailed in al-Hira and Iraq and fell under Sassanid Persian rule between 268 and 632; the Ghassanids in Syria and Palestine, who were ruled by Byzantium from 200 to 633; and the Kinda dynasty, which developed in Najd and was independent of both Persia and Byzantium (100 B.C. - 400 A.D.)

THE ISMAELI ARABS

The Ismaeli, or Adnani, Arabs are descendants of Ismael and of the prophet Abraham (*Ibrahim*). They became the most recognized and noteworthy of the Arab tribes because Islam emerged from amongst them.

According to tradition, the prophet Abraham emigrated, around 2000 B.C., from Mesopotamia to Egypt before reaching Makkah with his wife, Hagar, and their son, Ismael. Islamic texts relate the story of

Ismael, who, as a child, was stranded with his mother near Makkah. As Hagar desperately searched the desert for water to drink, she prayed to God to lead her to a place with drinking water. In response to her prayers, the angel Gabriel appeared and struck a hole in the ground, from which water started to flow. This water is believed to be the origin of the Zamzam Well in Makkah, which in Islamic tradition is considered sacred. Abraham's subsequent construction of the Kaabah, the house of God, in Makkah made the city a sacred place of pilgrimage, centuries before the advent of Islam. According to tradition, Ismael lived among the people of Makkah and married a woman from Jorhum; their union was the origin of the tribe of Quraysh.

Paved section of the old Hajj route from Yemen to Makkah.

THE QURAYSH TRIBE

Around the year 440, a man called Qussai bin Kilab became a prominent figure in Quraysh. He was the Prophet Muhammad's fourth great-grandfather and a direct descendant of Ismael. Thanks to his deep wisdom, Qussai was able to unify the tribe of Quraysh, which was previously torn apart by inner conflicts. He became a respected lord of Makkah and the guardian of the Kaabah.

Qussai bin Kilab had three children: Abdmunaf, Abduluzi, and Abduldar. The eldest son, Abdmunaf, became one of Makkah's elders and, with his brothers and sons, inherited and maintained Qussai's prestigious position as the Kaabah's custodian and guardian. Abdmunaf was responsible for the well-being of pilgrims, a task that was a source of great pride even in pre-Islamic times.

Hashem, Abdmunaf's son, undertook major trade journeys to neighboring lands on behalf of the Quraysh tribe. It is reported that he was the first to establish the biannual journeys that are well known in Quraysh's history as the Winter Journey (*rihlat al-shita*) to Yemen, and the Summer Journey (*rihlat al-saif*) to Syria. Upon his death, Hashem was succeeded by his brother al-Muttaleb, who was later succeeded by his son, Abdulmuttaleb. Abdulmuttaleb had ten children, one of whom was Abdallah, the Prophet Muhammad's father.

During the reign of Abdulmuttaleb, several developments took place which later proved of special significance. These included a growing sense of competition among the various tribes for the custodianship of the Kaabah. The rediscovery of Ismael's Zamzam Well, after its disappearance under the sands, and the historic Battle of the Elephant in 570 also had profound consequences.

The Battle of the Elephant occurred when Abreha, the king of Abyssinia (Ethiopia), invaded the Asir region and the city of Najran after the Abyssinian occupation of Yemen. He then decided to launch a military campaign against Makkah in order to destroy the Kaabah. Abreha's attempts failed and his troops withdrew, although they maintained a presence in Yemen for some time. That year became known in pre-Islamic times as the Year of the Elephant (*Sanat al-Fil*), a reference to the elephants the Abyssinians used in their assault. It then served as a reference year from which Arabs dated events for a period of fifty years.

Prior to Islam, the Arab tribes followed various religions and creeds. Some of them worshiped the stars and planets, others embraced Judaism or Christianity. The majority, however, worshiped idols which were placed in and around the Kaabah in Makkah.

The Arabs then had no religious institution that reconciled their various rites and creeds, nor a centralized state that unified their tribes and protected them. Each tribe adhered unyieldingly to its beliefs. However, during the annual holy truce the paths of religion and trade met. The tribes laid down their arms and entered Makkah, unified for a short time by one central precept: the glorification of the Kaabah and the competitive urge to serve it and adorn it. As such, the shrine served all the Arabian gods and was the sanctuary of more than 360 idols. Around the Kaabah the tribes not only erected their idols but also hung the best of their poetry. While the majority of the population of pre-Islamic Arabia was illiterate, many people cherished the oral tradition of poetry and prized literary eloquence.

The Emergence and Spread of Islam

The Prophet Muhammad was born in 571 (the year of the Battle of the Elephant) to Qurayshi parents. His father, Abdallah bin Abdulmuttaleb bin Hashem, died before he was born. His mother, Aminah bint Wahab bin Abdmunaf, passed away before he was six years old and left him in the custody of his grandfather. Muhammad was eight years old when his grandfather died, and he went to live with his uncle, Abu Taleb.

At the age of twenty-five, Muhammad was a trusted and highly regarded young man who undertook his first trading trip to Damascus, leading a caravan that belonged to Khadijah bint Khuwailid, one of Quraysh's most respected women. Khadijah chose him for this mission because of his renowned honesty. Shortly after his return from Damascus Muhammad married her and the two lived together until her death twenty-five years later. They had two sons, who did not live, and four daughters.

The Prophet Muhammad

When Muhammad was in his forties, he would leave Makkah briefly to spend days and nights meditating on nearby Mount Hira. In the middle of the month of Ramadan in 612, Muhammad received his first revelation through the angel Gabriel. At first he shared his revelations only with his wife and closest friends, then he proceeded to spread the Islamic faith. Among the first people who believed in the message proclaiming God the ultimate creator and the source of all knowledge were his wife Khadijah, his cousin Ali bin Abi Taleb, and his friend Abu Bakr, whom Muhammad called *al-siddiq* (the most truthful). Abu Bakr, a prosperous merchant, had abandoned his wealth for the cause of Islam. These three believers were followed later by other members of Muhammad's family and several Qurayshi elders.

Islam rejected polytheism and all forms of paganism, and called for the abolition of slavery and the establishment of a compassionate and socially responsible society. However, as the new religion gained popularity, it was met with overall hostility from most Qurayshis, who felt that their religious traditions and mercantile interests were threatened. The Qurayshi merchants, in particular, actively opposed it.

After spreading the word of Islam for more than ten years, Muhammad saw the believers in the new faith increasingly persecuted. Consequently, he encouraged some of his followers to seek refuge in Abyssinia, where they received generous treatment from its Christian king. As the early Muslims continued to be abused in Makkah, he sent some of them to the northern city of Yathrib, later to be renamed Madinah. At the time, Muhammad had gained support among the people of Madinah, who repeatedly invited him to move to their city and offered to protect him and his followers.

Learning of a Qurayshi plot against him, the Prophet left Makkah and moved to Madinah in 622. That year, called the Year of the Hijrah (emigration), marked the beginning of the Islamic calendar. In this regard, it should be noted that the Arabs subscribed to the lunar calendar even before Islam. A lunar year is composed of twelve months varying between twenty-nine and thirty days. The lunar year is eleven days shorter than the solar calendar year and, therefore, its cycles do not always correspond with the seasons.

Islam spread quickly among most of the residents of Madinah as well as to neighboring towns. Many Muslims also emigrated to Madinah from Makkah. Meanwhile, the Quraysh tribe was making desperate efforts to stop the spread of the new religion. Its troops fought Muhammad and his followers in several battles in which Muslims finally triumphed. In 629 Muhammad reentered Makkah with his supporters, spared the lives of his enemies, and won more converts among his most bitter opponents. Proclaiming the oneness of God, he took over the Kaabah and destroyed the idols and other symbols of paganism.

Three years after conquering Makkah without bloodshed, and accompanied by over a hundred thousand Muslims, Muhammad made his last pilgrimage to the Kaabah. There, he gave his historic farewell sermon and recited the last chapter (*surah*) of the Quran, announcing the end of God's revelation of the holy book. Upon his return to Madinah three months later, he suddenly fell ill and died on Monday, 8 June 632.

Islam and the Holy Quran

Islam, as revealed to the Prophet Muhammad, is based on the belief in one and only one God. In

Arabic, Islam means "submission" (to the will of God). It recognizes and endorses a long line of prophets inspired by God. Among them are Abraham (*Ibrahim*), Moses (*Musa*), David (*Dawud*), and Jesus (*Isa*). Muhammad is acknowledged as the last of all prophets, and the Quran, Islam's holy book, completes and seals all previous revelations. Islam is defined by what are known as the Five Pillars: the profession of faith (that there is no god but God, and Muhammad is His prophet); prayer five times a day; alms-giving (*zakat*); fasting during the month of Ramadan; and pilgrimage to "God's House" (the Kaabah) in Makkah by those who are able to make the journey. Islamic teachings are explained first in the Quran then in the Hadith and Sunnah (the Prophet's sayings and deeds). The Islamic provisions stated in the Quran can be divided into three parts. The first explains religious beliefs and creeds. The second covers dealings and relations among people, and between people and their leaders. The third set forth the social aspects of people's lives and the ethical and moral standards that enable the individual to lead a productive life in society.

THE RIGHTEOUS CALIPHS

Muslims received the news of Muhammad's death with shock and disbelief. Some were confused and disillusioned, forgetting the Prophet's last sermon and the verses in the Quran that refer to the death of prophets as all mortals. They learned also that Muhammad had not named his successor; instead, he left the issue of succession to be settled through consultation among his immediate followers. Abu Bakr, Muhammad's "most truthful" friend, was quick to dispell the confusion with an eloquent speech that pleaded with the people to worship not the mortal Muhammad, but the immortal and almighty God. Stressing the divinity of God and the humanity of Muhammad, he stated: "Whoever worshiped Muhammad should know that Muhammad is dead, but whoever worshiped God knows that God lives and dies not." The Muslim elders then met and elected Abu Bakr to be the successor (*khalifah*, anglicized as caliph), of Muhammad.

A devout Muslim as well as a firm and compassionate leader, Abu Bakr moved promptly to discipline those who seceded from Islam upon the Prophet's death. After winning the support of the remaining Arab tribes, he was able to unify them under the banner of Islam. Strengthened by their new faith, the Arabs now faced the two giants that had ruled the region for centuries: Byzantium and Persia.

Abu Bakr soon dispatched armies to conquer Iraq and Syria under the command of the great Muslim general, Khaled ibn al-Walid. Heraclius, the Byzantine emperor, led an army of 240,000 troops to face the advancing Muslim armies. Khaled ibn al-Walid scored a series of triumphs against the Byzantine army, the most decisive of which, the Battle of al-Yarmuk, enabled the Muslim forces to conquer Damascus, Aleppo, Latakia, and other coastal cities.

Iraq was conquered between 633 and 635 in two major battles—al-Hafir and al-Liss—in which Khaled ibn al-Walid scored a clear victory after fierce fighting. By the time Abu Bakr died in 634, Islam had become well established throughout the Arabian Peninsula.

Upon Abu Bakr's death, Omar ibn al-Khattab became caliph in compliance with a recommendation by Abu Bakr that Omar be his heir. Omar had been Abu Bakr's advisor and main aide and had served him skillfully and sincerely. During his term in office the Arab armies continued their advance and scored many victories over the Persians. One of the major battles was at Qadisiyah in 635, where Muslim troops had to face the elephants that the Persians used at the vanguard of their army. Although this was their first experience in battle with elephants, the Muslim forces succeeded in defeating the Persians and occupying Ctesiphon, the Persian capital.

In 637 Omar dispatched an army under the command of Amru bin al-Aas to conquer Palestine. The army swept through its coastal cities and for four months laid siege to Jerusalem. Its inhabitants, led by Patriarch Saphronius, insisted that they would surrender the city only to the caliph himself. To grant them their wish, Omar traveled to Jerusalem and signed a covenant pledging safety for its residents, thus gaining control of the city in 637. The tolerance shown by the treaty was characteristic of Islam and was to set a standard for generations to come.

Amru bin al-Aas marched from Palestine to Egypt. He conquered al-Arish and Bulaibis at the edge of the desert, advanced to the Nile delta region in 638, and in 641 marched on to Ain Shams and Alexandria. By the end of Amru's campaign, Egypt, which had been under Roman rule for centuries, became a province of the young Islamic Empire. On the eastern front, the city of Hamadhan and other Persian townships were brought under Islamic control during that same year.

Three days after Omar's death in 643, Othman bin Affan was elected caliph. Othman was a wealthy man who gave considerable amounts of money to the poor and the needy. During his term, he pushed forward with military campaigns, bringing more regions under Islamic control, including Azerbaijan, Tabarstan, the Caspian Sea area, and the island of Cyprus.

Under Othman's leadership and in cooperation with his cousin Muawiyah, the governor of Syria, the first Muslim fleet was built. It engaged the Byzantines in many sea battles and conquered the most important islands in the Mediterranean. Also during Othman's reign, all the verses of the Quran were collected from various sources. Until then, the Quran had been mostly committed to memory by trusted disciples, or partially copied onto loose parchment and wood tablets. A single text was then cross-referenced, agreed upon, and kept through the ages unaltered.

Ali bin Abi Taleb, cousin and son-in-law of the Prophet, assumed the duties of caliph after Othman was killed during a rebellion. A brave fighter and a man of letters, Ali was deeply religious and righteous. His rule, however, was plagued with turmoil. He was unable to capture those responsible for Othman's murder, despite his vow to bring them to justice. As a result, the legitimacy of his rule was challenged by Muawiyah, Syria's governor. The incidents of that period, including Ali's assassination in 661, caused serious divisions and disputes within the Muslim community.

The deaths of Othman and Ali resulted in an irreparable rift in the community of Islam, splitting it into two main groups: Sunnis (*ahl al-sunnah*) and Shiites (*shiah*). While Sunnis and Shiites agree on almost all the essentials of Islam, their most salient difference, more political than religious, pertains to the question of succession to the Prophet Muhammad. The Sunnis, who represent the majority of Muslims, affirm the selection of the successor through an elective process; the Shiites, on the other hand, believe that the succession must be hereditary and therefore remain in the family of the Prophet. In addition, the Sunnis regard the caliph as the keeper of the religious laws, while the Shiites see their leader, the *imam*, as a recipient and interpreter of the Prophet's knowledge and spiritual message.

THE UMAYYADS AND THE TRANSFER OF THE CALIPHATE TO DAMASCUS

Following Ali's death, Muawiyah was proclaimed and accepted as the new caliph. During his reign Damascus became the new capital of the Islamic Empire, replacing the Hijaz as the political center of Islam. Muawiyah was an exceptional politician and an able administrator who was admired for his strength, restraint, and tolerance. But although he moved quickly to suppress various disturbances around the empire, he was, until his death in 677, unable to resolve the conflict with the Shiites. From Damascus, the Umayyads ruled the Islamic Empire for ninety-one years and conquered many lands, each with an established cultural and artistic heritage. The Umayyad rulers sought to live up to the standards of these old cultures and incorporated the ancient classical traditions in their new life style.

One of the most prominent Umayyad caliphs was Abdulmalek bin Marwan, who assumed power in 685. Important public projects were undertaken during his reign, including dredging and clearing waterways that irrigated the valleys between the Euphrates and Tigris rivers, thus increasing agricultural production in the region. In addition, the taxation system was restructured; Islamic gold coins were minted to replace the numerous currencies in use; postal services were improved and reorganized; and throughout the distant provinces of the Empire, Arabic became the official language of the state, replacing Greek and Pahlavi.

Although the history of the central region of the Peninsula in this era is unclear, it is believed that Najd was a province of the emirate of Iraq, and that Asir was annexed to the emirate of the Hijaz or of Yemen.

Started in 687 and completed in 691, the Dome of the Rock, one of the most important Islamic mosques, was built in Jerusalem. Constructed around the rock from which Muhammad is believed to have ascended on a journey to heaven, the mosque was erected to replace a more modest structure that was built fifty years earlier by the caliph Omar ibn al-Khattab.

It is evident that in constructing their mosques and other buildings in the conquered regions, Muslims were very much influenced by the prevailing architectural designs and arts. The Dome of the Rock, also known as the Mosque of Omar, was no exception; with the intricate mathematical relationships underlying its design, the mosque represents a true synthesis of the architectural styles of those times. To this day, it stands as one of the jewels of Islamic architecture.

Other major mosques, such as the Umayyad Mosque in Damascus and the al-Aqsa Mosque in Jerusalem, were built in 705 during the era of the Umayyads. Under al-Walid bin Abdulmalek, the Hijaz witnessed one of its most magnificent periods. Al-

Walid appointed his cousin, Omar Abdulaziz, governor of Madinah and Makkah, and the new governor emulated the style of his maternal grandfather, Omar ibn al-Khattab. He appointed well-known jurists and scholars (*ulama*) as his advisors. In 706, acting on a directive from al-Walid, he ordered the expansion and reconstruction of the Prophet's Mosque in Madinah. Omar Abdulaziz also rebuilt the central water well that served as the major source of drinking water for the people of Madinah. In addition, he paved the main route that linked Madinah with Makkah.

Islam continued to grow quickly and expand into new regions during the Umayyad period. The Islamic conquests reached northern India with the occupation of the Sind and Punjab provinces in 710. This

Restored al-Kharabah reservoir, Darb Zubaidah. Northeast of the city of Taif.

began the era of conquest of the rest of the Indian subcontinent, the Far East, and parts of China in the following decades. To the west, North African tribes began to convert to Islam. Starting from Morocco, Islam spread across the Mediterranean into Spain's Andalusia in 707-708 and through northern Spain to the French city of Narbonne in 713. In 728 Islam reached its northernmost point—the Loire River, some 170 miles from Paris. In 732 the advancing Muslim army was finally stopped, by the French commander Charles Martel, in the Battle of Poitiers.

The arrival of Islam in Andalusia ushered in one of the most brilliant periods in human civilization. Spectacular advances were made in all branches of science (medicine, astronomy, chemistry, and mathematics) and the humanities (philosophy, literature, poetry, and music). Andalusia's major cities developed at an unprecedented pace. Cordoba's population, for example, reached 500,000; it boasted 700 mosques, 70 libraries (one housed 500,000 volumes), and 900 public baths. Granada, Seville, and other cities witnessed similar progress and development. Characterized by a spirit of great religious and intellectual tolerance and justice, the Umayyad period was one of the brightest chapters in Islamic history.

After the death of Hisham bin Abdulmalek, the last great Umayyad caliph who ruled from 724 to 743, four weak caliphs, in rapid succession, came to power.

It was during the reign of Marwan II that the Umayyad dynasty faced its ultimate challenge. In 747 a well-organized group of rebels, with strong alliances in Khorasan and Iraq, brought down the Umayyad dynasty and transferred the caliphate to Abu al-Abbas al-Saffah, a descendant of the Prophet.

The Abbassids and the Transfer of the Caliphate to Baghdad

Abu al-Abbas al-Saffah is credited with the establishment of the Abbassid dynasty in 745. Twelve years later, the Abbassids made Baghdad their capital. During the early days of their reign they followed the administrative norms established by the Umayyads, and soon became more committed to trade than to war. Al-Saffah appointed his uncle, Ziad bin Abdallah, governor of Madinah, Makkah, Taif, and Yamamah. The Bahrain province, which included what is now Saudi Arabia's Eastern Province, was later annexed to the Hijaz governorate by the second Abbassid caliph, Abu Jaafar al-Mansur.

In 756, during al-Mansur's reign, new quarters were added to the Grand Mosque in Makkah. Two more expansions of the Grand Mosque were ordered during the reign of al-Mahdi (774-785) whose wife, al-Khaizaran, acquired land during her pilgrimage to Makkah and had several new mosques built in that city.

Under Harun al-Rashid, who became caliph in 786, great progress was achieved in the arts, sciences, technology, and agriculture. Unparalleled innovations were also made in banking in order to meet the needs of an ever-expanding trade network. Baghdad became one of the most vibrant cultural centers in the world. Scientific and political delegations were exchanged with some European countries, and goods and merchandise were traded with China and India.

During the reign of Harun al-Rashid, the people of Makkah and Madinah enjoyed an era of prosperity. The Caliph went on pilgrimage to Makkah almost every year, and each time he ordered the expansion and improvement of the mosques. Al-Rashid's wife, Zubaidah, started major projects to improve traveling conditions along the pilgrimage routes. She also had water supplied to Makkah from Ain Hanin, a nearby spring, as well as to the Hajj sites of Arafah and Mina from a source named after her in the Numan Valley.

The Abbassid caliphs accomplished a great deal in the Hijaz area. However, most of the development projects were limited to the two holy mosques in Makkah and Madinah and the routes leading to them; other parts of the Hijaz were left undeveloped.

Toward the end of Harun al-Rashid's reign, the Empire was proving too large to govern from a centralized capital. The strong hand that once held an empire of scattered and diverse provinces and tribes was now slowly losing control. Northern Africa was no longer under Abbassid rule when al-Mamun, the son of Harun al-Rashid, became caliph. Although al-Mamun was probably the greatest of the Abbassid caliphs, the decline which began before his arrival continued.

The beginning of the thirteenth century witnessed the Arab loss of city after city in Spain and the capture of Jerusalem by the Crusaders. But the final blow was yet to come. In 1258, the remaining signs of Abbassid rule finally disappeared following a brutal Mongol invasion led by Hulagu Khan. After having invaded parts of central Asia, Russia, and central Europe, the Mongols overran the Arab armies, entered Baghdad, destroyed the city and its irrigation systems, burned its schools and libraries, and decimated its population. The invasion added to the pre-existing problems and stripped the Abbassids of their leadership position, turning their Empire into one of the world's most destitute areas. Never in history had a civilization suffered such a sudden and devastating blow.

THE OTTOMAN TURKS AND THE TRANSFER OF THE CALIPHATE TO CONSTANTINOPLE

The Ottoman Turks were tribes who were originally driven out of their homeland in the central Asian plains near the Caspian and Aral seas by the Mongols. They adopted Islam as their faith and settled in Asia Minor. Artugrul, the first chief of the Ottoman confederation, was succeeded by his son Othman, after whom the Ottomans were named. In 1326 the Ottomans captured the city of Bursa and made it their capital.

Under Sultan Muhammad II, also known as "The Conqueror," the Ottomans occupied Constantinople in 1453, after having extended their conquests into Greece and Albania. During the sixteenth century, the Ottomans proved their organizational skills by devising a centralized administrative network which enabled them to control an extraordinarily diverse and vast empire.

The Ottoman rule in the Hijaz started in 1517 when Sultan Salim I received the keys to the two holy mosques at Makkah and Madinah. He is said to be the first Ottoman caliph to place the *kiswah* (the traditional black covering) on the Kaabah.

Salim I was succeeded by his son, Sultan Sulaiman ("The Magnificent"), in 1520. Sulaiman's good deeds earned him the title of *al-qanuni* ("the lawmaker"). Such actions included the renovation of the Kaabah's roof in 1552, the building and strengthening of Jeddah's walls, and the completion of a water main that extended Ain Zubaidah's water supply from Mina to Makkah. He also assigned Makkah and Madinah additional annual funds.

Sulaiman's heir, his son Sultan Salim II, began ruling the Ottoman Empire in 1566. Following in his father's footsteps, he finished renovating Makkah's Grand Mosque. Salim II also replaced the existing wooden roofs over the colonnades with more durable stone domes and arches. Four centuries later his legacy lives on.

During the reign of Sultan Ahmad I (1603-1617) a structural defect threatened the Kaabah. The sultan's religious advisors disapproved of his wish to demolish and rebuild the Kaabah and urged him instead to reinforce its structure. He followed their advice and had gold-plated copper bands installed around it. The sultan's other accomplishments included furnishing the Prophet's chamber in the Madinah mosque with valuable gifts and ornaments.

In 1629, a devastating torrential flood swept through the Grand Mosque and caused several serious cracks in the walls of the Kaabah. After consulting the *ulama*, the Ottoman Sultan Murad IV decided to tear down and rebuild the entire edifice. This was the first and only time the Kaabah was rebuilt since Islam's early days.

After Murad IV, the Ottoman sultans' attention turned to containing domestic unrest and enemies beyond their borders. Towards the begining of the eighteenth century, chaos spread to the whole Empire and power came into the hands of regional governors and tribal chiefs. In 1798, following France's invasion of Egypt it became increasingly evident that the Ottoman Empire was in decline. While the Ottomans were trying to consolidate their presence in the Arabian Peninsula, the area was about to enter another phase of its history.

THE KINGDOM OF SAUDI ARABIA

Although no documented history of Najd in the early eighteenth century is available, it is well known that this period, during which the House of Saud started to gain prominence, was marred by on-going warfare throughout the Arabian Peninsula. This was the result of many years of internal chaos and conflict stemming from the Ottomans' inability to control their vast Empire.

Local governors eventually tightened their grip on the towns while trying to contain the rebellious bedouins. During this period the tribe was the ultimate social unit, and the tribal shaikh enjoyed undisputed leadership. Some tribes were roaming nomads constantly in search of water and pasture. Others settled in oases and villages, although their life styles and values were still influenced by their nomadic roots.

SHAIKH MUHAMMAD BIN ABDULWAHAB'S CALL TO REFORM

In matters of religious beliefs and practices, the early eighteenth century was also an era of ignorance and misguidance. Heresy, sedition, and superstition, which are far from the spirit of Islam, were very common throughout the Peninsula. Several jurisprudent shaikhs stood up in the face of heretical practices and anti-Islamic traditions, calling for strict compliance with the Quran and the Prophet's teachings. Shaikh Othman bin Ahmad al-Najdi (died in 1687), a noted Muslim theologian, was known in Najd before the appearance of Shaikh Muhammad bin Abdulwahab. Al-Najdi subscribed to the Hanbali tradition of Islam and was deeply concerned with religious reform. The reformist movement, however, did not gain prominence until the emergence of Shaikh Abdulwahab.

Shaikh Muhammad bin Abdulwahab was born in 1703 in the town of al-Uyaynah, north of Riyadh. His grandfather was a religious judge (*qadi*) and his father one of al-Uyaynah's notables. During his early years Shaikh Muhammad studied the Quran and Islamic jurisprudence and was an avid reader of Hadith and Quranic exegesis. He moved to Makkah and Madinah to study under some of the cities' most renowned religious scholars. He returned to Najd after spending some time in Basrah, Iraq, and in al-Hasa on the Gulf. Shaikh Abdulwahab was dismayed to see the Arabian Peninsula being crushed by the Ottoman iron fist, and the ignorance, impoverishment, and decadence it brought with it. He was especially concerned about the destructive effects of those conditions on the religious spirit of Islam. He believed in the need to return to the basic teachings of the Quran, but like most reformers, he was met with opposition. He fled his hometown to seek refuge in the oasis town of al-Diriyah, near modern-day Riyadh, where he was welcomed by its ruler, Muhammad bin Saud.

THE HOUSE OF SAUD

The House of Saud was named after its founder, Saud, the first son of Muhammad bin Muqrin of the Inazah tribe. Saud's headquarters were in al-Diriyah, about eight miles west of Riyadh. Al-Diriyah was one of the Peninsula's strongest and most important emirates at the time and later became the first capital of the House of Saud. Saud established and expanded his rule in all the oases around his capital during the eighteenth century.

Saud's son, Muhammad bin Saud, was known to be a cunning and shrewd politician. He was also a devout Muslim angered by the deterioration of religious fervor and the disunity and enmity that had grown among the people. The meeting of Shaikh Abdulwahab and Muhammad bin Saud was a historic event. The two men understood each other and saw in their cooperation the dawn of a new era for the Arabian Peninsula. In 1740 bin Saud vowed to lend all his support to the reformist movement of the Shaikh, and to this day, the two men's pledge of cooperation is considered one of the most important events in the Peninsula's modern history.

Political might, coupled with religious renewal, gave bin Saud a leading edge in consolidating his rule over wide areas of the Peninsula. By the time of his death in 1765 bin Saud had conquered most of Najd and had won overwhelming support for the religious reform movement. His son Abdulaziz, who had been raised in the reformist movement founded by his father's friend and ally, succeeded him.

Shaikh Muhammad bin Abdulwahab died in 1791. People viewed him with respect as a reformist whose lifetime goal was to return the Islamic community to the purity of Islam. He wrote several books on the roots of Islam and the oneness of God. He was, and still is, a great source of inspiration to religious scholars.

Abdulaziz bin Muhammad bin Saud, also a deeply religious leader, was very active, even before his father's death, in spreading the reformist movement. He had led his father's forces in several campaigns all over the Peninsula and won the allegiance of many tribes. At the beginning of the nineteenth century, and under his leadership, Saudi rule spread north to the banks of the Euphrates, east to Ras al-Khaima and Oman, west to the Hijaz, and south to Asir. In 1803, Abdulaziz was assassinated in the al-Diriyah Mosque and was succeeded by his son, Saud bin Abdulaziz.

The reign of Saud bin Abdulaziz, also known as Saud the Great, brought prosperity to the House of Saud. His experience as commander of his father's army and as his chief advisor in expanding Saudi control and supporting religious reform served him well. But the Ottoman government, the Egyptians, and the shaikhs of the Hijaz feeling threatened by the Saudi resolve, sought to discredit it by accusing the Najdi ruler of starting a new religious sect.

As a result, the House of Saud faced a vicious campaign of religious vilification with negative consequences that persisted for many years. However, by the time war broke out between the Saudis and the Ottomans together with their Egyptian allies, Saud the Great had subdued a major part of the Arabian Peninsula as well as various regions in Iraq and Syria. One of his most celebrated achievements was the total conquest of the Hijaz, and assumption of the role of custodian of the two holy mosques of Makkah and Madinah. Saud died in al-Diriyah in 1814.

During his reign, Saud bin Abdulaziz entrusted to his son, Abdallah, the command of several punitive expeditions into various areas of the Peninsula. Three years before Abdallah assumed power, Muhammad Ali Pasha, the Ottoman governor of Egypt, had started a military campaign against the Najdi rulers. In two years the Egyptian armies were able to expel the Najdi forces from the Hijaz, but it took them seven years to subdue the House of Saud in its heartland, Najd, and to overtake al-Diriyah. The prolonged warfare caused the Najdi and the Turkish-Egyptian armies substantial losses.

Indeed, Abdallah bin Saud's tribal support and political wisdom were not enough to defeat the huge and well-equipped army of Muhammad Ali Pasha. In 1818 the Egyptian army surrounded al-Diriyah, and after stiff resistance seized the city and completely destroyed its houses, mosques, and orchards. Abdallah bin Saud and other members of his family surrendered to the governor of Madinah. They were sent to Egypt and then to Constantinople, where they were put to death.

The Egyptian army also took control of the holy mosques in Makkah and Madinah and the region of Asir. Instead of returning these areas to the direct rule of the Ottomans, Muhammad Ali placed them under his control and independently governed them for a quarter of a century, until he was forced to withdraw his armies in 1840.

During the siege of al-Diriyah, Saud's cousin, Turki bin Abdallah bin Muhammad bin Saud, was in the Kharj Province. Upon receiving news of the fall of the Saudi capital, he returned to the city of al-Arid, where he engaged in a power struggle with his cousin Muammar, the prince of al-Uyaynah. Turki wrested control from Muammar then took on the task of fighting the Ottoman-Egyptian forces with the aid of his son Faisal. In 1823 he mounted a counterattack and was able to recapture al-Diriyah and Riyadh. He was the first member of the House of Saud to declare Riyadh his capital. Indeed, he was able to expel the invaders from Najd and restore most of what was Saudi territory before the Ottoman-Egyptian invasion. Turki's first task was to unify the ranks of the tribes still loyal to the House of Saud. After ruling for ten years he was assassinated by his cousin Mishari bin Abdulrahman bin Saud, who had hoped to seize power from him.

When his father was assassinated, Prince Faisal bin Turki led an army of supporters against Mishari, and in 1833 defeated him and reclaimed power. Faisal then resumed the struggle against the Ottomans, fighting them for nine years before his surrender to Khorshid

Pasha, the Ottoman army's commander, who took him captive to Egypt.

Later, Faisal was pardoned and returned to lead the House of Saud until his death in 1865. At that time, his four sons were holding key political positions: Muhammad governed the Northern Province; Saud ruled al-Kharj and al-Aflaj; and Abdallah was responsible together with Abdulrahman, the fourth and youngest son, for Riyadh. The four brothers fought bitterly over the throne. Their rivalry sapped the energy of the House of Saud, which made it easier for Muhammad ibn al-Rashid to gain control of their lands.

To be sure, Faisal's death ushered in a new phase in the history of the House of Saud, one marked by local rebellions and internal fighting. Muhammad Ali Pasha's strategic support of the al-Rashids, who had established their political base in Hail, balanced the power of the House of Saud in Najd and so facilitated Muhammad Ali's continued control of the Hijaz. When the Ottoman government decided to extend its domination to other areas of the Arabian Peninsula, it focused its efforts on bringing ibn al-Rashid into its sphere of influence. The al-Rashids did not resist because they needed Ottoman help to confront their traditional enemies—the House of Al Saud and the House of Al Sabah in Kuwait.

After his attempt to recapture al-Hasa, Faisal's second son, Saud bin Faisal, attacked the tribe of Otaibah near Riyadh. He engaged in a fierce battle against ibn Rubayan, one of the Otaibah notables, and was seriously wounded and taken to Riyadh, where he died in 1874.

Faisal's third son, Abdallah, returned to Riyadh upon his brother Saud's death. After a series of attempts to expand his power base in the region, he tried to recapture the al-Hasa region from the Ottomans, but he failed. He succeeded, however, in taking over the town of Unaizah, though he met with fierce resistance from the inhabitants of Buraydah. Its inhabitants eventually solicited support from Muhammad ibn al-Rashid in Hail, who was only too glad to oblige by breaking Abdallah's siege, and seizing the town for himself. At this time, Abdallah lost hope of gaining political power. He moved to Hail and lived there for one year, then returned to Riyadh, where he died in 1889.

Abdallah's brother, Abdulrahman bin Faisal, spent his years in power trying to end the hegemony of Muhammad ibn al-Rashid. But despite his wisdom, courage, and administrative skills, his attempts were unsuccessful. He was dealt a final blow at the battle of al-Mulaydah, in the Qassim region, in 1891. Isolated, Abdulrahman sent his family to Bahrain to seek the protection of its ruler, who was his personal friend. Unable to reorganize his forces, he later traveled to Qatar, Bahrain, and in the end took refuge with his family in Kuwait. Abdulrahman did not go back to Riyadh until 1906, when his son, Abdulaziz, recaptured the city from the al-Rashid clan.

When Abdulrahman bin Faisal was forced to leave Riyadh for Kuwait, ibn al-Rashid appointed Abdulrahman's brother, Muhammad bin Faisal, governor of Riyadh. However, ibn al-Rashid allowed Muhammad very limited power, cleverly using him as a figurehead and disguising his own control of the city. In the meantime, ibn al-Rashid tried his best to gain acceptance and establish direct rule over Riyadh.

When Muhammad bin Faisal died, ibn al-Rashid decided not to replace him with another member of the House of Saud. At this time it seemed that the presence and power of the House of Saud in the Arabian Peninsula had vanished completely.

However, when ibn al-Rashid was about to savor his victories a young warrior from the House of Saud came out of exile in Kuwait, and embarked on a historic journey that restored power to the House of Saud and paved the way for the birth of the modern Kingdom of Saudi Arabia.

Abdulaziz bin Abdulrahman al-Faisal Al Saud was born in Riyadh in December 1880. The House of Saud had then been weakened by internal strife, and seen its hold on power in the Najd region deteriorate. In his youth Abdulaziz had witnessed his uncles' bitter fights over the succession to the throne; he had also noted the House of Saud's consequent loss of power to Muhammad ibn al-Rashid. Likewise, he was deeply saddened by his father's forced withdrawal from active political life and his de facto exile in Kuwait.

Abdulaziz lived in Kuwait with his father and family for ten years. This was a turbulent period both in Najd and Kuwait. In Najd Muhammad ibn al-Rashid was using brutal means to establish his dominance over the various tribes. The fires of disunity and infighting were fueled by a fierce struggle for power in the Arabian Peninsula between the Ottomans and the British. Abdulaziz followed these developments closely, while learning valuable lessons from Kuwait's ruler, and waiting for the opportunity to reclaim the lost power of the House of Saud.

In 1902 Abdulaziz's forces took over Riyadh twice in one year. Four months after they seized it the first time, they were driven out by al-Rashid's men. However, soon afterward, Abdulaziz went back to Riyadh with no more than forty warriors and was able, in a remarkable raid, to recapture it. Welcomed by its population, Abdulaziz lost no time in building the necessary fortifications around the city to prevent another setback. Riyadh soon became a center of power that went so far as to cover the entire area now known as the Kingdom of Saudi Arabia.

THE BIRTH OF THE KINGDOM OF SAUDI ARABIA

During the reign of Sultan Abdulhamid II, the Ottoman Empire was threatened by hostile Russian armies from the east and by European territorial ambitions from the west. In order to counter these threats, Abdulhamid worked on consolidating his power in every way. At home he built forts, military bases, government halls, and hospitals in Makkah, Madinah, Taif, and other cities. One of Abdulhamid's greatest accomplishments was the completion of the 800-mile Hijaz Railroad between Damascus and Madinah.

At the regional level, Abdulhamid called for the creation of an Islamic league in an effort to rally the Arabs under the Ottoman caliphate's banner. Further, he followed a policy of supporting Arab leaders who were willing to accept Ottoman hegemony and cracking down on those who resisted. Such a policy cost Abdulhamid dearly in the Arabian Peninsula; all his campaigns into Asir, Yemen, and Najd had catastrophic results. His attempts to support ibn al-Rashid against the House of Saud were crowned with failure when in 1909 ibn al-Rashid was defeated. In the end, Abdulhamid's self-serving strategies led to the birth of liberation movements calling for independence from the Ottomans.

Among the anti-Ottoman movements that emerged in the Arabian Peninsula in the final years of the Ottoman sultanate were those led by al-Idrisi in Tihamah and Asir, and Imam Yahya in Yemen. Meanwhile, Sultan Abdulhamid II was deposed and, in Turkey, a constitutional government was formed. Soon the new rulers removed Sharif Ali Pasha from power in Makkah, and in 1908 replaced him with Sharif Hussain ibn Ali, who was seeking to consolidate his rule in the Hijaz. Born in Makkah, Sharif Hussain had lived mostly in Istanbul, yet he was committed to preserving his family's rule in the Hijaz. In an attempt to win the Turkish government's favor, he led an Ottoman-backed attack against al-Idrisi, who had laid siege to the city of Abha. Sharif Hussain also conducted similar offensives against areas controlled by the House of Saud.

These campaigns did not deter Abdulaziz from asserting and expanding his rule in Najd. In 1913 he led his army eastward and defeated the al-Hasa Turkish garrison, capturing the province and other Arabian Gulf areas.

During World War I the Arab struggle against the Ottoman Empire intensified. Sharif Hussain announced the birth of the Arab Revolt and, siding with the allies, he fought the Turkish forces. At the end of World War I, Ottoman rule of the Arabian Peninsula came to an end, leading to the rise of five independent Arab governments: the Hijaz Kingdom, the Najd Sultanate, the al-Rashid Fealty, the al-Idrissi Emirate, and the al-Aed family Emirat.

In 1921, after a three-month siege, Abdulaziz conquered Hail and soon occupied the Jauf Province in the north. One year later Abdulaziz dispatched an army under his son Faisal's command to put down a rebellion in Asir that was supported by the Hijazis. Faisal was able to subdue Abha, Asir's capital, bringing the whole area under the House of Saud.

In 1924, when Sharif Hussain proclaimed himself king of all the Arabs, Abdulaziz sent an army to occupy Taif, as a first step toward controlling the Hijaz. In one year, Abdulaziz managed to take over Jeddah, Makkah, and the rest of the Hijaz. Early in 1926, he announced the unification of Najd and the Hijaz, declaring himself "King of the Hijaz and Sultan of Najd and its Dependencies." When Abdulaziz annexed the al-Idrisi's lands of Tihamah and Asir, his title was then changed to "King of the Hijaz, Najd, and its Dependencies." At the time he used Riyadh and Makkah as his two capitals.

Five years later, on 22 September 1932, after a series of administrative reforms needed by the growing new central government, Abdulaziz issued a decree proclaiming the birth of the "Kingdom of Saudi Arabia."

ANCIENT ROUTES

Left: *Camel herd.*
Great Nafud Desert, 150 miles southeast of the city of Riyadh.
The camel was domesticated around 2500 B.C. Known for its endurance, it made the desert caravans possible. Camel herds are still prized for their hair, milk, and meat and remain a symbol of wealth for many bedouins.

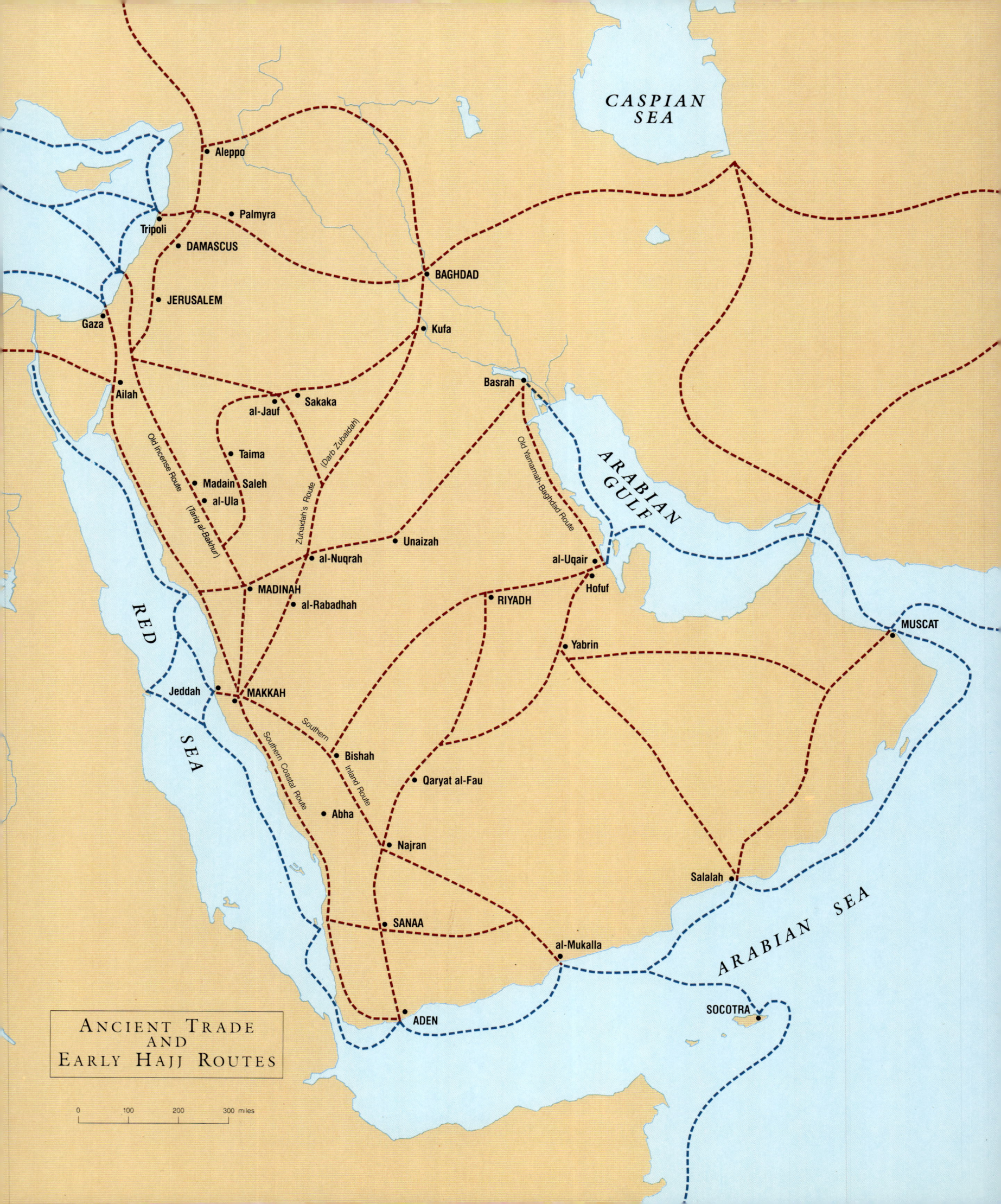

Ancient Routes

Ancient Trade and the Arabian Peninsula

The Arabian Peninsula lies between Asia and Africa and is separated from them by the Arabian Gulf to the east and the Red Sea to the west. To its south lies the Arabian Sea. Due to this privileged geographic location, the Arabian Peninsula has served since early times as a passageway for migrating peoples, a meeting point between East and West, and an important stopping place on trade routes, even before the advent of Islam.

Throughout the ages, the Arabian Peninsula was a center for shipping and trading activities. This led to the development of many routes that connected the coastal regions with inland cities and other neighboring areas.

The Role of the Peninsula Before Islam

Researchers believe that the Arabian Peninsula was home to various peoples, civilizations, and city-states that emerged contemporaneously. In addition to trading with each other and with civilizations outside the Peninsula, they engaged widely in social, economic, and cultural exchanges.

Archaeological discoveries in the northeastern part of the Peninsula show evidence of trading activities between Mesopotamia and the Arabian Gulf as far back as 5000 B.C. Other data evince commercial relations with China and with the Mediterranean countries in the north.

Sumerian inscriptions dating as far back as 4000 B.C. refer to the people of Magan (believed to be present-day Oman) as shipbuilders and traders who carried goods, including iron and copper, from Magan to Mesopotamia.

Commercial activities among these people ebbed and flowed. It would seem that around 2000 B.C., direct trade relations between Magan and Mesopotamia receded. Goods exported from Magan began to be unloaded at ports in Dilmun (present-day Bahrain); they were then re-exported to their final destinations.

Egyptian ships had been traveling the Red Sea to southern Arabia since 2500 B.C. During that period, the vessels that made such journeys were built at the mouth of the Gulf of Suez. They would sail down the Red Sea to its southernmost point and then return loaded with frankincense, a much-desired incense; and myrrh, a resin that was a valuable ingredient in ancient perfumes, medical preparations, and embalming substances. The ships also carried back pine wood and glue, materials essential for shipbuilding.

The introduction and utilization of metals prompted Ramses III (1198-1167 B.C.) to dispatch a fleet of large ships to take over the copper mines in the Sinai Peninsula. An American team that was exploring the area of Tell al-Khulaifah (west of Aqaba) in 1938-1940 discovered the remains of a city in which it found a large copper mining and smelting site, iron and copper nails, pieces of thick rope, and quantities of tar and glue for coating ships. Archaeologists therefore have deduced that Tell al-Khulaifah could have been used as a mining and shipbuilding site by the Egyptians.

Due to the expansion of commerce on the Red Sea, the trade routes on the Arabian Gulf lost prominence for some time. However, the discovery of archaeological sites in Oman dating back to around 1000 B.C. has led to the conclusion that, by that time, some level of business activity and prosperity had returned to the Arabian Gulf region.

With the rise of the Assyrian civilization in Mesopotamia and the re-emergence of the Indian civilization around the year 700 B.C., trade relations among India, Mesopotamia, Oman, and the Arabian Gulf region continued to expand. Faced with competition from the Phoenicians on some trade routes, the Assyrian king, Sinharib (705-681 B.C.), destroyed the city of Tyre in order to reduce trade through the Red Sea and revive commercial ventures in the Arabian Gulf. Until then, the Phoenician city-states of Byblos, Sidon, and Tyre had prospered in linking the trading markets of the Peninsula, Egypt, Cyprus, Anatolia, and the western shores of the Mediterranean.

Shipping activities along the Gulf surged under the governance of the modern state of Babylon (629-539 B.C.). The Persians opened new horizons for economic development after they conquered western Asia and Egypt and built a large empire during the reign of Cambyses (522-521 B.C.). Parts of India were overtaken under the Persian monarch Darius I (550-486 B.C.), and trade relations with the east were expanded. Darius I recognized the importance of establishing solid trade links between his empire and India and Egypt by sea, as well as by land. To that end, he dispatched a fleet that set sail from the Sind River and journeyed to the Gulf, around the coast of the Arabian Peninsula, on to the Red Sea, and finally to Egypt. It is also believed that Darius I re-opened an ancient pharaonic waterway that linked the Red Sea with the Mediterranean. This canal, which probably originated at one of the branches of the Nile near the city of Zaqaziq, passed through the valley of Tumilat, Timsah Lake, and the Great Bitter Lake to reach Suez. It measured an impressive eighty miles from beginning to end.

Largely influenced by the social and economic conditions of the states in the region, shipping activities between the Arabian Gulf and the Red Sea prospered at times and faltered at others. Trade routes also changed according to political and military factors, which caused the emergence of some cities and the decline of others.

After the rise of the Greek civilization and the occupation of Egypt, Alexander the Great (356-324 B.C.) ordered his commander, Dinocrates, to build the city of Alexandria (332 B.C.). This led to a substantial increase in trading activity between the Mediterranean and the Red Sea. When Alexander expanded his empire to southwestern and central Asia in the early third century B.C., maritime trade between the Gulf area and the east (including present-day India and China) witnessed great expansion. The Gulf merchants imported gold, silver, silk, and precious stones, including lapis lazuli, ivory, and carnelian, from those areas.

Having prevailed over Egypt and Greece's old trading rival Phoenicia, Alexander led his armies against Persia, determined to avenge earlier Greek defeats. In three years, his lightning eastern drive conquered all of the Persian Empire and reached India.

For the first time in history, an empire stretched from the Atlantic shores of North Africa to the Indus River. A vast array of cultures came under a single yet highly decentralized rule, and a common Hellenistic currency was in use.

In keeping with the changes surrounding them, the people of Arabia had by that time developed a network of roads that linked their ports and stretched inland across the Peninsula. Finding themselves in the middle of an unprecedented and most lucrative trading market, the southwestern Arabian kingdom of Saba and the northwestern Arabian kingdom of Nabatea prospered.

Soon after Alexander died, his lieutenants and regional governors jousted for power, thus dividing and weakening the Hellenic Empire. As Greek hegemony declined, the world witnessed the birth and rise of Rome.

After a century-long attempt to gain full control over the Mediterranean trade routes, Rome finally succeeded, in 146 B.C., in crushing the Phoenicians and destroying Carthage, their capital. Having secured its western trade routes and markets, Rome began to look toward Egypt, the Arabian Peninsula, and the trade routes to the east.

Following the conquest of Egypt in 25 B.C., the Roman emperor Octavian Augustus (63 B.C.-14 A.D.) decided to extend Rome's hegemony over the Red Sea and Arabia. Backed by the Roman senate, Augustus ordered the governor of Egypt, Aulius Galius, to lead

Rome's Egyptian legion down the Red Sea coast of Arabia. The 1,400-mile expedition was aimed at establishing control over the area that produced Arabia's famed riches.

From Cleopatris, an Egyptian port facing present-day Yanbu in Saudi Arabia, the legion was ferried across the Red Sea on galleys specially built for the passage. Traveling overland, the expedition reached the Yemeni walled city of Marib six months later. Seeing his troops exhausted by an extreme climate and decimated by hunger, sickness, and accidents, Aulius Galius ordered them to retreat, not knowing that he was within reach of the riches of *Arabia Felix*.

After the failure of the Arabian expedition, Augustus extended Rome's influence along the African coast of the Red Sea. He established friendly relations with the ruling dynasty of Aksum, which controlled northern Abyssinia and the Eritrean coast. It was an alliance that lasted generations.

At the same time, Rome turned its attention to the Arabian kingdoms that controlled the trade routes between the northern part of the Peninsula, Syria, and the Mediterranean. As their influence grew the Romans built new roads to facilitate their expansion and better control trade. One of these roads, constructed around the year 106, had markers erected along it that read "Via Nova A Finibus Syria Usque Al Mare Rubrum," meaning, "The New Road from the Syrian Border to the Red Sea." It connected with other roads from the Arabian Gulf in the east and from Yemen in the south.

With the expansion of the Roman Empire, harbors all around the Peninsula benefited from new trade opportunities and prospered. Ships sailed into their waters for loading and unloading goods or for repairs. On the Red Sea, some of the northernmost active seaports included Myus Hormus on the Egyptian shores, and Leuce Come on the Arabian shore.

The Greek geographer and historian Strabo (66 B.C.-19 A.D.) wrote that at the peak of the sailing season at least 120 vessels sailed daily from Myus Hormus. On the southern coast of the Red Sea lay the Arabian port of Mokha and the Abyssinian port of Adulis. Facing the Indian Ocean, Eudaemon (Aden) and Cane offered safe haven to the ships that sailed across the ocean from India. Closer to the coast of the Indian Ocean, the island of Dioscorida (Socotra) was an active trade center where Indian, Arab, Persian, and African merchants met and exchanged goods.

At the entrance to the Arabian Gulf, Oman became a thriving port. Further north lay the island of Tylus, the city of Gurrah (present-day al-Uqair)—which was one of the most important trading centers in the area—and the ports of Teredon, Apologos, and Charax.

The Roman historian, Pliny the Elder (79-32 A.D.), also wrote a detailed account of the Arabian Gulf coast and its surrounding areas. He mentioned Oman and other prosperous cities and described their inhabitants and trading activities. Pliny also noted that the boards of Arab ships were tied together by ropes made of coconut fibers, a practice still seen today in some Arab dhows. He praised the skills of Arab seamen and documented their utilization of northeastern monsoon winds in their journeys to India.

The Arabian Peninsula's exports included myrrh, frankincense, incense, silver, and gold. India traded precious stones, spices, silk, cotton, manufactured gold

Nabatean rock-carved tomb, Madain Saleh. Northwest of the city of Madinah.

and silver items, ornaments, and wood. Fur, silk, embroidery, precious stones, and colored pottery were imported from China, and ivory, leather, and wood came from the eastern coast of Africa. Aware of the overwhelming Persian influence in the Gulf and having failed to conquer southern Arabia, the Romans became more interested in the Peninsula's northern trade routes.

In 106, during Emperor Trajan's reign (98-117), the northern Arabian kingdom of Nabatea was occupied and became a Roman province. Having firmly secured the northwestern trade routes to Egypt, the Romans annexed the desert trading city-state of Palmyra (*Tadmor*) in 120, thus effectively gaining control of the northeastern trade routes to the Gulf.

While the Nabatean Roman province gradually disintegrated, Palmyra slowly but surely regained its importance and, for a while, its independence. In the third century, the power of Palmyra, led by the Arab queen Zenobia, extended from the heart of the Syrian desert to Asia Minor, Mesopotamia, and Egypt. In 272, Rome's might was unleashed against the prosperous city-state. The Roman troops invaded Palmyra, captured Zenobia, and put an end to Palmyrene independence. As a result, the frontiers between the Roman and Persian empires were drawn in northern Arabia, with smaller client states emerging as a buffer between the two giants.

The advent of the fourth century saw Christianity spreading beyond the boundaries of the Roman Empire. The kings of Abyssinia had converted, and pockets of Christianity were established even in southern Arabia. In 340 an attempt by the king of Saba to impose Judaism over the area triggered an Abyssinian campaign. Aided by the Romans, the Abyssinian troops crossed the strait of Bab al-Mandab and occupied all of southern Arabia for thirty-five years and the Yemeni coastline sporadically thereafter.

Perceiving the Abyssinian presence and Roman gains as a challenge to the southern trade routes, the Persians reinforced their presence in Oman, consolidated their relations with the neighboring Arab tribes, and developed a new alliance with the Himayrites, who had been overthrown by the Abyssinian invasion. As in the northern part of the Peninsula, the Persians and Romans competed with each other through client-states in the south.

Surrounded by the two giants, a small, independent, and polytheistic state, called Kinda, expanded during that time in southern Najd. Its influence grew rapidly and reached the coastlines of the Arabian Gulf and the Red Sea. Prior to vanishing around the fifth century A.D., Kinda had developed a highly sophisticated culture that was nurtured by the state's own economic and political power.

While the entire Peninsula was about to suffer for over a century from the struggle for supremacy between Persia and Rome, a number of small caravan cities, including Makkah and Yathrib (Madinah), continued to develop as independent trading centers. Located along the main caravan routes and inhabited by tribes accustomed to the rigors of desert life, Makkah became the Peninsula's thriving trade capital.

Ancient Land Routes

One of the most important roads in the Arabian Peninsula, known as the Incense Road (*Tariq al-Bakhur*), started as several roads on the coasts of Hadramaut and Yemen. Some of the roads met at Marib, joined others in Najran, then split again into two roads. The first became the Yamamah-Baghdad road and led to al-Fau, Kinda's ancient capital. From there it extended to al-Kharj, then further east to al-Hasa and along the eastern coasts of the Arabian Gulf until it reached southern Iraq. The other branch of the Incense Road led to Taif, Makkah, Madinah, al-Ula, and Madain Saleh, where it branched into two roads: one went to Taima, Sakaka, and then to al-Najaf in Iraq; and the other, a continuation of the Incense Road, continued to Tabuk and Petra, and from there to Egypt, Syria, and further west.

Another significant roadway started in Hadramaut and ran along the Red Sea coast to Tihamah, where it met the Incense Road.

Additional roads linked the Arabian Gulf to the Mediterranean, including one that started in Jurrahah (present-day al-Uqair), passed through al-Kharj (close to where Riyadh is today), and continued north to Unaizah. From Unaizah a branch crossed the Nafud Desert to Jubbah and Dawmat al-Jandal and continued to Damascus. Another branch reached Taima and joined the northern section of the Incense Road, heading toward Petra.

The Eastern Road, linking Oman to Iraq, began in Oman and extended to the Yabrin Oasis and al-Kharj, where it joined the roads coming from Najran and Marib. Before Islam, Qurayshi merchants traveled some of these roads in their legendary summer journeys to Syria and winter journeys to Yemen. After the emergence of Islam, the Arabs took full control over the coasts of the Arabian Peninsula. They consolidated and unified their political power over the various regions and utilized these roads as an integrated system that linked all parts of the Peninsula.

During the Abbassid period (750-1258) the Arabian Gulf acquired special significance as the closest sea gate to India and China. Trade with these countries reached its peak; indeed, the two most important cities in the world at the time were Baghdad, the capital of the Abbassid Empire, and Changan, the Chinese capital known today as Xiah. Called the Silk Route, the road between these two major cities, estimated at 7,000 miles, was considered the longest at the time.

During the zenith of the Abbassid dynasty, merchandise from all over the world poured into Iraq. Basrah, which was a cultural and commercial center before Baghdad gained prominence, was the most important port in the Arabian Gulf. An extensive transportation network of land, sea, and river routes intersected at Basrah. Its central market, al-Mirbad, was an international meeting place for merchants and for men of letters as well. There, goods from all over the world were traded: lynxes, elephants, tigers, leather, musk, ambergris, rattan, camphor, cloves, coconut, and precious stones from India; silk, quality fabrics, paper, ink, peacocks, perfume, fine tools, and marble from China; lead, dyes, and spices from Kirman; iron and arms from Khurasan; pearls from the Arabian Gulf shores, Oman, and Socotra; sapphires, diamonds, and pearls from Sarandib; wool, fox hide, and rugs from Azerbaijan; produce, arms, iron, and silk fabrics from Syria; horses, camels, and leather from the Arabian Peninsula; incense and myrrh from Yemen; papyrus, fabrics, donkeys, medicines, turquoise, and some precious metals from Egypt; and lynxes, falcons, wool fabrics, and mats from North Africa.

The Abbassid caliphs clearly recognized the importance of trade. They encouraged trade relations within and outside their borders and paid special attention to the development of land and sea routes. To Egypt and the Byzantine Empire, they exported metalwork, especially copper plated with gold and silver, in addition to flour, barley, rice, fruits, herbs, grains, fabrics, oils, licorice, and extracts of roses, jasmine, violets, and saffron.

THE HAJJ ROUTES

Throughout the ages, millions of devout Muslims from all over the world have crossed land and sea routes to make their annual pilgrimage to Makkah. *Hajj,* as the pilgrimage is called in Arabic, is one of the Five Pillars of Islam. The pilgrimage to the Grand Mosque in Makkah must be undertaken at least once in the lifetime of any able Muslim. It is an individual as well as a collective spiritual experience that takes place during the second week of the twelfth month (*Dhu al-Hijjah*) of the Muslim lunar year.

Some of the early roads used by the pilgrims traversed hostile terrain and remote and deserted areas. In order to make the journey easier for them, successive caliphs paved the most difficult portions of these roads and erected identifying markers that indicated the distances to specific destinations. The Hajj routes followed some of the same trade routes known before Islam and were invariably named after their lands of origin.

The route that linked the Iraqi city of Kufa to Makkah was long considered the most important among the Hajj routes. Constructed during the rule of Caliph Abu al-Abbas, it was later known as the Zubaidah Route (*Darb Zubaidah*), in honor of the wife of Caliph Harun al-Rashid, Zubaidah, who had arranged for water to be provided for the pilgrims through the construction of an extensive system that included catch-basins, cisterns, pools, and wells. Along its 900-mile path, the road had fifty-four main and secondary rest stations. At al-Nuqrah the road divided; one section headed toward Madinah and the other toward Makkah.

The road from Damascus to Makkah proceeded inland, passing through Busra al-Sham, Tabuk, and Madinah and from there to Makkah.

The Egyptian Hajj route, starting in Fustat (old Cairo) and crossing the Sinai Peninsula to Ailah

Rain storm along Darb Zubaidah. East of the city of Makkah.

(present-day Aqabah), ran parallel to the Red Sea until it reached Yanbu, then turned east toward Madinah.

Another major Hajj route originated in Hadramaut and Yemen and headed northward. In Aden it divided into two branches: a coastal roadway on the Red Sea and a mountainous one that passed through the town of al-Juwah, where a grand mosque built in the ninth century still exists today.

CARAVANS AND TRAVEL STATIONS

Domesticated around 2500 B.C., the camel was known for its endurance, which made the desert caravans possible. Merchants rented caravans from tribal shaikhs, whose profession was caravan outfitting and organization. Caravans consisted of camels and pack animals, and were led by experienced guides to their destination. These professional organizers charged the merchants specific sums of money for the services provided during the trip. Part of the money was paid to tribal leaders on caravan routes; another part was reserved for wages of caravan guards.

The caravan shaikh acted as the main guide and, like a ship's captain, had full control over the caravan. Some caravans made several stops in cities along the way, while others embarked on non-stop journeys. Caravans would grow larger as other, smaller ones joined them along the way.

The cargo on caravans was covered with special cloths that protected it against desert conditions and then tied down with ropes made of palm or hemp fibers. The number of camels carrying goods varied according to the nature of the caravan, the type of merchandise it transported, and the trading conditions in the cities of origin and destination. In the case of major caravans, the number of camels ran into the thousands. Larger caravans tended to travel slowly, averaging seven hours a day, and some of the longer journeys took several months.

Caravans stopped at specific locations that offered water, provisions, resting places, and facilities for worship. Some of the stations offered protected grazing areas (*hima*). In addition to their water resources, certain stations were renowned for the lushness and variety of their pastures. The remains of some of these stations, such as the extraordinary site of al-Rabadhah, located east of Madinah, are the focus of a major research effort at present.

European Trading Activities with the Orient

After the collapse of the Abbassid caliphate, the end of Islamic dominance in Spain, and the rise of the Ottoman Empire, Western interest in finding new routes to the Orient in order to control trade with India and China increased. The discovery of the sea route around the Cape of Good Hope by Vasco da Gama in 1498 was a turning point in European trading activities; as a result, the military and maritime strength and standing of the Portuguese in the Indian Ocean were greatly enhanced. Ironically, it was the well-known Omani captain, Ahmad bin Majed, who led Vasco da Gama's ship from East Africa across the Indian Ocean to Calcutta, thus unwittingly helping to end the Arabs' dominance at sea.

In 1506, the Portuguese sailor Alfonso de Albuquerque led a fleet of five ships in an attempt to halt commercial traffic on the Red Sea and disrupt the trade route that crossed through Egypt to Venice. He captured the island of Socotra as well as several Arab ports, including Aden and Muscat. These successes encouraged the Portuguese to attempt to capture Jeddah, but the Ottomans intervened in southern Arabia, broke the Portuguese sea blockade, and reclaimed Yemen in two maritime campaigns in 1519 and 1538.

The Portuguese were followed by other colonial powers with similiar aims in the area—first the Dutch, then the British, and finally the French. As their frigates began to sail along the new route to India, they created small outposts along the Arabian coast of the Indian Ocean. The rapid increase of Western influence in the Orient and the fierce competition among European countries undercut the Arabs' advantage along their land and sea routes. Gradually, control over trade with the Orient was transferred from Arab to European hands.

The Hijaz Railroad Between Damascus and Madinah

Until the turn of the twentieth century, pilgrims who traveled the Syrian Hajj route between Damascus and Madinah spent approximately a month and a half on the road before reaching their destination. In 1900 the Ottoman sultan, Abdulhamid, decided to upgrade the Turkey-Madinah Hajj route by building the Hijaz Railroad between Damascus and Madinah. While the project effectively assured the Ottomans better control of Arabia, its announced objective was to ease the burden of the pilgrims' journey. In order to finance its construction, contributions were solicited from Muslims worldwide and special committees were formed to collect donations in several countries. By the time the project was launched, 750,000 Ottoman gold pounds had been collected. The building of the 800-mile track took eight years. For the pilgrims, the completed Hijaz Railroad was an impressive accomplishment: its trains allowed pilgrims to travel in relative comfort and complete the trip in four days.

During World War I, the British officer T.E. Lawrence led a contingent of Arab forces against the Ottomans. He blew up the Hijaz Railroad and its facilities at several sites in order to cut the supply route of the Ottoman army. The railroad track, which was originally planned to extend all the way to Makkah, has not been in operation since that time.

Archaeological Research

Very few accounts of early travels to Arabia go as far back as those of the 12th century chronicler Ibn Jubayr. Born in Spain to a family that had migrated four centuries earlier from the Hijaz, he undertook in 1183 a one-year journey that led him from Granada, to Alexandria, Jeddah, Makkah, Madinah, and Baghdad, before returning home to Spain.

Another Arab traveller, Ibn Battuta, travelled from his native Tangier to Egypt, Syria, and Palestine, before reaching Makkah in 1326. The story of his three pilgrimages to the Holy Cities, and of his travels to every Muslim land of his time, were recorded in great detail by Muhammad ibn Juzay.

Western Travellers

Among the few recorded early western travels to Arabia is the journey that was undertaken in 1503 by a Portuguese man named Lodovico de Varthema. Passing as a Muslim, he traveled from Damascus to Madinah, Makkah, the southern shores of Arabia, and then to Persia and India. He was the first westerner to visit and describe the Holy Cities of Islam.

In the early eighteenth century, the Orient that fascinated Europe was not the Far East of India and China, but the closer territories of the Ottoman Empire. Egypt, Palestine, Syria, and the Arabian Peninsula held an attraction that was rooted in centuries of romantic tales and mysteries. Until then, the West's interest in the area had been expressed largely through trade, occasional diplomatic exchanges, and an incipient historical and scientific curiosity.

It was in the midst of this burgeoning fascination with the area that a pioneering German traveler, Carsten Niebuhr, published a voluminous account in 1772 of a journey that took him from Turkey to Iraq, Egypt, and Yemen. This remarkable volume was published first in German and later in French and English. It included detailed maps and illustrations of places and people that few other European travelers had encountered before.

Napoleon's incursions into Egypt in 1798 were followed by a surge of interest in the region. In 1807 a Spanish traveler set foot in Jeddah under the assumed name of Ali Bey al-Abbassi. Posing as a Muslim descendant of the Abbassid caliphs, he managed to tour several cities on the Red Sea. He later located cities such as Yanbu and Jeddah on geographic maps, as well as the positions of Makkah and Madinah on the world map.

Two years later, the Swiss-English traveler Johann Ludwig Burkhardt began his travels in Syria. Burkhardt (known by his alias Shaikh Ibrahim bin Abdallah) had studied Arabic, the Quran, and Quranic exegesis. He succeeded in entering the two holy mosques in Makkah and Madinah and wrote a detailed description of the Hajj season. In 1812 he discovered the vestiges of the forgotten city of Petra, in Wadi Musa. Burkhardt published several books on his travels in Syria, Palestine, and Arabia. He died in Cairo and was buried there.

A few years later, in 1822, a French professor named Jean-Francois Champollion unveiled the secrets of the Egyptian hieroglyphic alphabet. A passionate fascination with the lands of Arabia reached new peaks in the West as a result of Champollion's research.

The Exploration of Arabia

In 1834 the British started their exploration of the Arabian Peninsula. James R. Wellsted visited several areas and unearthed important remains and ancient inscriptions. He was followed in 1853 by another British traveler, Richard Burton, who traveled the pilgrims' route.

France also began to show interest in researching the archaeology of the Middle East. The Paris-based Academie des Lettres et Beaux Arts published a series of studies on Semitic inscriptions and sent the Orientalist scholar J. Halevy on a mission to several areas that included Marib, al-Jauf, and Najran. Halevy returned to France with many ancient inscriptions. His greatest discovery, however, was the remains of Carna, the capital of the Minean dynasty.

A few years later, in 1876, Charles Montague Doughty trekked from Damascus to Palestine and Jordan. He later joined a caravan of pilgrims and began his travels in the Arabian Peninsula.

The Austrian Orientalist Sigfrid Langer also traveled to Arabia during the same period. He was a specialist in the Arabic language and copied several Himayrite inscriptions.

Dr. and Mrs. Theodore Bent journeyed to Bahrain and Oman in 1889. They visited several archaeological sites and wrote extensively about their travels.

The scientific expeditions came to a temporary halt during World War I (1914-1918). However, when the war ended the travels resumed with a renewed interest.

The British traveler Bertram Thomas, who served as finance minister in the government of the sultan of Muscat, crossed the Empty Quarter in 1931 and discovered Lake Milhah. Harry St. John Philby, also known as Abdallah Philby after he converted to Islam in 1952, continued Thomas' expeditions and traveled throughout the Arabian Peninsula during the reign of King Abdulaziz. In 1932 he traveled from Hofuf to the Jabrin (*Yebrin*) Oasis and then headed south toward the Empty Quarter. He advanced to the city of al-Sulayyil and then to Wadi al-Dawaser, Najran, and Asir, before reaching Hadramaut.

Philby, one of the most active Western travelers in the Arabian Peninsula, published many accounts of his journeys. He also verified the locations of some cities whose existence was uncertain, such as al-Uqair, or ancient Jurrahah, on the eastern coast of the Kingdom and the lost city of Wabar in the Empty Quarter. He died in Beirut, Lebanon, in 1960.

In 1962 an American expedition trekked through several regions in the Kingdom, including Sakaka, al-Jauf, Taima, Tabuk, Madain Saleh, and al-Ula. The American team's important discoveries included ancient pottery and Thamudic and Nabatean inscriptions.

To protect its valuable heritage and to nurture scientific research in archaeology, the Kingdom of Saudi Arabia created in the early 1960s the Saudi Department of Antiquities. This was followed by a royal decree that instituted the High Council for Antiquities, which was charged with establishing the national policies and programs governing the preservation and study of Saudi antiquities.

The University of Riyadh, now known as King Saud University, has shown a deep-seated commitment to archaeological research. It encouraged the founding of the Society of History and Archaeology in 1969 and became an active supporter of the initial excavations at Qaryat al-Fau in 1972. The university further formalized its commitment to scientific and archaeological research by creating, in 1978, the Department of Archaeology and Museology.

Over the years, several valuable research projects have been conducted throughout the Kingdom in cooperation with well-known international scholars and institutions. However, three impressive projects, all led by Saudi scholars, best exemplify the pioneering work of Saudi archaeology and herald the plethora of potential discoveries still to be made.

The earliest of these projects comprises the research and excavation work sponsored by King Saud University at Qaryat al-Fau and directed by Professor Abdulrahman al-Ansari, chairman of the Department of Archaeology and Museology. Located approximately 440 miles southwest of Riyadh, the site is yielding a wealth of information and is believed to contain the remains of the capital of the ancient state of Kinda (100 B.C. - 400 A.D.).

Another valuable undertaking was a survey, conducted in 1975, of all reported historical sites in the Kingdom. Headed by Dr. Abdullah H. Masri, director of Antiquities and Museums, the survey reached some of the most remote areas of the Kingdom and represents a most valuable record of Saudi Arabia's partially uncovered heritage.

A more recent project, also sponsored by King Saud University, is the archaeological work begun in 1979 at al-Rabadhah. The site is an early Islamic settlement located approximately 130 miles east of Madinah. It was one of the numerous caravan stations established along Darb Zubaidah, the ancient road used by pilgrims which crossed the desert from Iraq to Makkah. This fascinating site was identified as a result of the trenchant work undertaken by the respected Saudi geographer and historian, Shaikh Hamad al-Jasir. The archaeological research and excavation team was led by Dr. Saad al-Rashid, a noted specialist in Islamic archaeology from King Saud University.

DRAWINGS AND INSCRIPTIONS

Archaeological surveys conducted throughout Saudi Arabia have recorded numerous sites with historical drawings and inscriptions. Spanning the centuries, they stand as eloquent witnesses of past civilizations. The discoveries generally can be grouped into two broad categories: ancient drawings and pre-Islamic inscriptions, and Islamic inscriptions.

Some of the ancient drawings and pre-Islamic inscriptions, left exposed to extreme weather conditions, have lost much of their detail. Fortunately, however, a surprisingly large number of sites have been able to survive the elements. Because of the inherent resilient qualities of granite surfaces, some of the better preserved work was found on granite rocks.

In many cases, the chiseled drawings and inscriptions stand out clearly against the naturally oxidized bluish-brown tones of granite.

Ancient drawings have been found in several locations throughout the Kingdom. While primitive in character, their stylized renditions resemble other prehistoric drawings found in parts of Africa and Europe. But unlike most of the European drawings, which are usually found in caverns, the majority of those discovered to date in the Kingdom appear on rocks and cliff sides. Most were carved on rock either in simple lines or as inscribed areas within clearly defined lines. Many comprise representations of the animals which once roamed the region, such as lions, lynxes, giraffes, ostriches, and African deer, and of animals which still exist today, like mountain goats, camels, horses, and various species of birds.

Drawings inside caves were sketched with hematite, a native anhydrous ferric oxide, and can be found in black, red, or orange. Some of the most beautiful compositions are found in Jabal Nier, twenty miles northwest of the town of Makhwat. Depicted within a wide crevice in a large granite rock formation, the drawings are approximately 18 x 6 feet and are rendered in hematite red. They represent men and women, as well as spotted animals with horns of wild cows and goat-like faces.

The drawings are characterized by unique designs that include images of camels. Human forms are depicted standing next to or mounting camels; usually they carry spears, sticks, or knives and await their prey. Some drawings show humans mounted on riding animals and chasing gazelles or mountain goats. Others represent humans standing alone, holding a large dagger or a spear or attacking a lion with arrows and shields. The gender and age of the human figures are usually indistinguishable; there are a few exceptions, however, such as the drawings of Jabal Nier and the compositions chiseled on a huge rock in Wadi Hirjab near the town of Samakh, fifty miles south of the city of Bishah.

Despite their simplicity, most of the pictures are full of life and movement. The artists' deep insight and skill provided a genuine and enduring expression of their people's daily existence and relationship to nature.

Pre-Islamic inscriptions were generally chiseled into the surface of the rock; some of them were relief-like. While numerous sites continue to be identified and researched, the majority of already-studied inscriptions include various ancient Arabian scripts. Among them are Thamudic inscriptions found on an outcrop near Madain Saleh; Lihyanite inscriptions carved on a rocky boulder in Wadi Ekmeh, near al-Ula; and Taimanite Thamudic inscriptions on the walls of a watchtower near the ancient city of Taima. Also noteworthy are the Nabatean inscriptions found at Rawwafah, southwest of Tabuk, and the large Sabaean engravings discovered on the walls of the Ukhdud temple in Najran. A wealth of inscriptions still waiting to be deciphered have been found throughout the peaks and valleys of Asir.

Successive forms of Arabic scripts have been identified in many areas, thus marking the advent of Islam in those locations. The evolution of the scripts as well as their contents provide us with valuable information about previous generations. Among the most important discoveries are the tombstones inscribed with the early undotted Kufic style of Arabic, dating back to the dawn of Islam.

Indeed, tombstones provide valuable data about the history of the Arabian Peninsula. In studying the development of Arabic calligraphy and its floriation and etching techniques, tombstones can offer a wealth of information about the names, titles, lineages, places of residence, and travels of the dead. Sometimes these grave markers also include names of the calligraphers and stonecutters and a description of their works.

Most of the tombstones were made of granite or basalt rock quarried in neighboring hills. These stones were frequently kept in their natural form. Often found on Hajj routes, many tombstones contain information about people who died on their way to or from the pilgrimage.

Islamic calligraphy on rocks or stones was either chiseled or executed in relief style. Some of the writings are difficult to read due to the intertwining of letters or their partial erosion by the harsh elements that eroded some of their parts over time. Others are still intact and easily comprehensible; their clear lettering and beautiful floriation testify to the skill and artistry of the early calligraphers.

Right: *Camel and oryx figures, about 12 to 28 inches high, chiseled on a rock.*
Village of Jubbah, 55 miles northwest of the city of Hail.
Below right: *Detail, approximately 12 inches high, of mounted warrior.*
Village of Jubbah.
Below: *Chiseled early Musnad script, with figures of warriors waving swords and shields. A nearby camel appears to be harnessed and saddled.*
Village of Jubbah.
Opposite: *Chiseled figure of a cart driven by two horses, about 18 inches high.*
Village of Jubbah.

The Heritage of The Kingdom of Saudi Arabia

Preceding overleaf: *Chiseled figures of antelopes, gazelles, lions, and ostriches. Also visible are hunters riding on camels and horses.*
Al-Musaiqrah, near the town of al-Quwayiyah, 88 miles west of the city of Riyadh.
Right and below: *Pillars of Rajajil.*
Rajajil, near the city of Sakaka.
  These 6- to 9-foot-high stone slabs are believed to be ancient markers dating to approximately 200 B.C.
Opposite: *Chiseled figures and Thamudic inscriptions.*
Al-Milahiyah, 25 miles southeast of the city of Hail.

THE HERITAGE OF THE KINGDOM OF SAUDI ARABIA

Preceding overleaf: *Chiseled palm trees, animal figures, and inscriptions in Thamudic Najdi script on a rock approximately 10 feet long.*
Jabal Yatib, southeast of the city of Hail.
Right: *Figures from various periods chiseled on a rock formation.*
Fifty miles west of the town of al-Muzahimiyah.
Below: *Chiseled hunting scene and inscriptions.*
Jabal Barnas, near the city of Sakaka.

ANCIENT ROUTES

Left: *Antelope figures chiseled on a rock.*
Fifty miles west of the town of al-Muzahimiyah.
Below: *Battle scene between two mounted warriors.*
Village of Jubbah, about 55 miles northwest of the city of Hail.

51

Below: *Granite boulder sheltering rare examples of figures painted on rock and dated to the second millennium B.C. Jabal Nier, 25 miles west of the town of al-Baha.*
Right: *Detail of rock panel painted with red hematite showing horned bovid and humanoid figures, the latter with belt sashes and swords at the waist. The triangular faces with feathered hair or head pieces, the long curved stick fingers and bowed lower bodies suggest that they may represent deities or participants in a ritual ceremony. The full panel includes other similar figures and is approximately 15 feet wide and 5 feet high.*
Jabal Nier.
Following overleaf: *Humanoid figures, approximately 9 to 12 feet high, lightly outlined on a large boulder. The highly stylized, 21-foot-wide drawing is unlike any other found and clearly includes representations of men and women.*
Wadi Hirjab, village of al-Samakh, 60 miles south of the city of Bishah.

Left: *Details of sun symbol and bird-like figures.*
Wadi Khdar, about 150 miles southeast of the city of Abha.
Below: *Lightly chiseled figures, approximately 3 feet high, on symmetrically split boulders. The arm silhouettes are brandishing scimitar-like swords. The triangular masks or faces are either sacrifice symbols or ritual representations.*
Wadi Khdar.
Right: *Chiseled figures with early south Arabian Musnad script.*
Zalakh Alia, near of the town of Sarat Abaidah, southeast of the city of Abha.
Following overleaf: *Chiseled inscriptions in south Arabian Musnad script.*
Sakhrat Shabar, near the village of Yadamah, 90 miles northeast of the city of Najran.

ANCIENT ROUTES

Left: *Inscriptions in south Arabian Musnad script. Tuwaiq escarpment, south of Qaryat al-Fau, 475 miles southwest of the city of Riyadh.*
Below: *Bas-relief inscriptions with figure, approximately 18 feet tall, believed to be that of an ancient deity named Kahl. Tuwaiq escarpment, south of Qaryat al-Fau.*
Right: *Ruins of Qaryat al-Fau, the ancient capital of the state of Kinda.*

Active between the second century B.C. and the fifth century A.D., Qaryat al-Fau was an important trade center in the heart of the Arabian Peninsula. Its past role as a pivotal trading capital was forgotten for generations, because its influence declined prior to the advent of Islam.

The site was first discovered in the forties by an ARAMCO team. It was later visited in 1952 by an expedition led by Harry St. John Philby, and in 1969 by the Belgian scientist Albert Jamme.

A scientific evaluation of the site was conducted in 1971 by the University of Riyadh, and was followed in 1972 by a series of excavations that have yielded a wealth of archaeological discoveries.

ANCIENT ROUTES

The Heritage of The Kingdom of Saudi Arabia

Below: *Escarpment on the edges of the Empty Quarter Desert, replete with ancient drawings.*
Jabal Thaer, about 65 miles north of the city of Najran.
Right and far right: *Chiseled figures of animals and a hunter. With a sword at his waist, the hunter appears to be holding a spear in his right hand and a bird in his left hand. The drawing clearly depicts the hunter's eyes and nose, as well as what appears to be a necklace.*
Jabal Thaer.

ANCIENT ROUTES

Below: *Chiseled figures of warriors riding horses and camels. Jabal Thaer.*
Bottom: *Figures of women chiseled over earlier south Arabian Musnad script inscriptions. Jabal Thaer.*

The Heritage of The Kingdom of Saudi Arabia

ANCIENT ROUTES

Left: *Horse figure and foot imprint chiseled on stone wall. Ancient temple of Ukhdud, city of Najran.*
Right: *Stylized Sabaean inscriptions chiseled on the walls of the Ukhdud temple.*
Below right: *Two intertwined snakes chiseled on a stone block. Ukhdud temple.*
Below: *Remains of the interior walls of the Ukhdud temple.*

   The large border around the slab reflects a stone-cutting technique unique to the region. The lower uneven rows of stone foundation have been exposed as a result of soil erosion.

   A lush oasis located on the western edge of the Empty Quarter Desert (Rub al-Khali) Najran was an important caravan center and a first-millennium A.D. Christian city. While much remains to be discovered about Najran's pre-Islamic sites, the scale of the Ukhdud archaeological remains confirms the historical importance of the city as described in early Sabaean and Roman texts.

Preceding overleaf: *Birkat Abu-Salim, the eastern water reservoir at al-Rabadhah, about 130 miles southeast of the city of Madinah.*

The caravan route that linked the Iraqi city of Kufa to Makkah, constructed during the reign of the Abbassid caliph Abu al-Abbass, was long considered the most important among the Hajj routes. It was later named Darb Zubaidah, in honor of the wife of Caliph Harun al-Rashid, Zubaidah, who arranged for water to be provided for the pilgrims through the construction of an extensive water retention system at each stop.

At al-Rabadhah, which was one of the most important stops along the route's 900-mile path, running rain water was channeled into a rectangular pool through a system of inlets and dams. There water was filtered by sedimentation. When the pool was full, the water overflowed into the circular reservoir. With a diameter spanning 190 feet and a depth of over 14 feet, sealed limestone walls, and a gypsum floor, the reservoir provided an essential supply of water for the rest stop.

The site was initially located and evaluated in 1978 by a team from King Saud University. The first season of full-scale archaeological research began in 1979.

Right: *Paved section of Darb Zubaidah.*
Birkat Kharabah, 100 miles northeast of the city of Makkah.
Below: *Old well along Darb Zubaidah.*
Al-Muwaih, 120 miles east of the city of Taif.

ANCIENT ROUTES

Left: *Well along the old southern caravan route, known as the Elephant Road (Darb al-Fil).*
 Town of Sarat Abaidah, southeast of the city of Abha.
Below: *Section of the old southern caravan route. Following certain dry stream beds, caravans ascended from Coastal Tihamah to the Asir highlands.*
 Qahr al-Anz, southwest of the city of Dhahran al-Janub.
Following overleaf: *Aquaduct, probably built during the late Ottoman era.*
 East of the city of Makkah.

ANCIENT ROUTES

Left: *Paved section of the old southern caravan route. Shab Ghalan, near of the town of Sarat Abaidah.*
Right: *Well along the old caravan route of Coastal Tihamah. Village of Harub, east of the city of Jizan.*
Below: *Well and marker along the old road from Jeddah to Makkah.*
   The inscription on the side indicates that the well was built during the reign of King Abdulaziz bin Abdulrahman Al Saud in 1365 A.H. (1945 A.D.).

Preceding overleaf: Old road ascending from Coastal Tihamah, along Wadi Hali, to the peaks of Jabal Salb.
Wadi Hali, west of the city of Abha.
Below: Non-punctuated early Arabic Kufic script chiseled on a rock that marks the burial site of a pilgrim along the old Hajj route from Yemen to Makkah.
Wadi Hirjab, village of al-Samakh, 60 miles south of the city of Bishah.
Right: Paved section of Darb al-Fil.
Al-Ashar, southwest of the city of Dhahran al-Janub.
Below right: Non-punctuated early Arabic Kufic script marking the burial site of a pilgrim along the old Hajj route from Basra to Makkah.
Town of al-Nabhaniyah, north of the city of Riyadh.

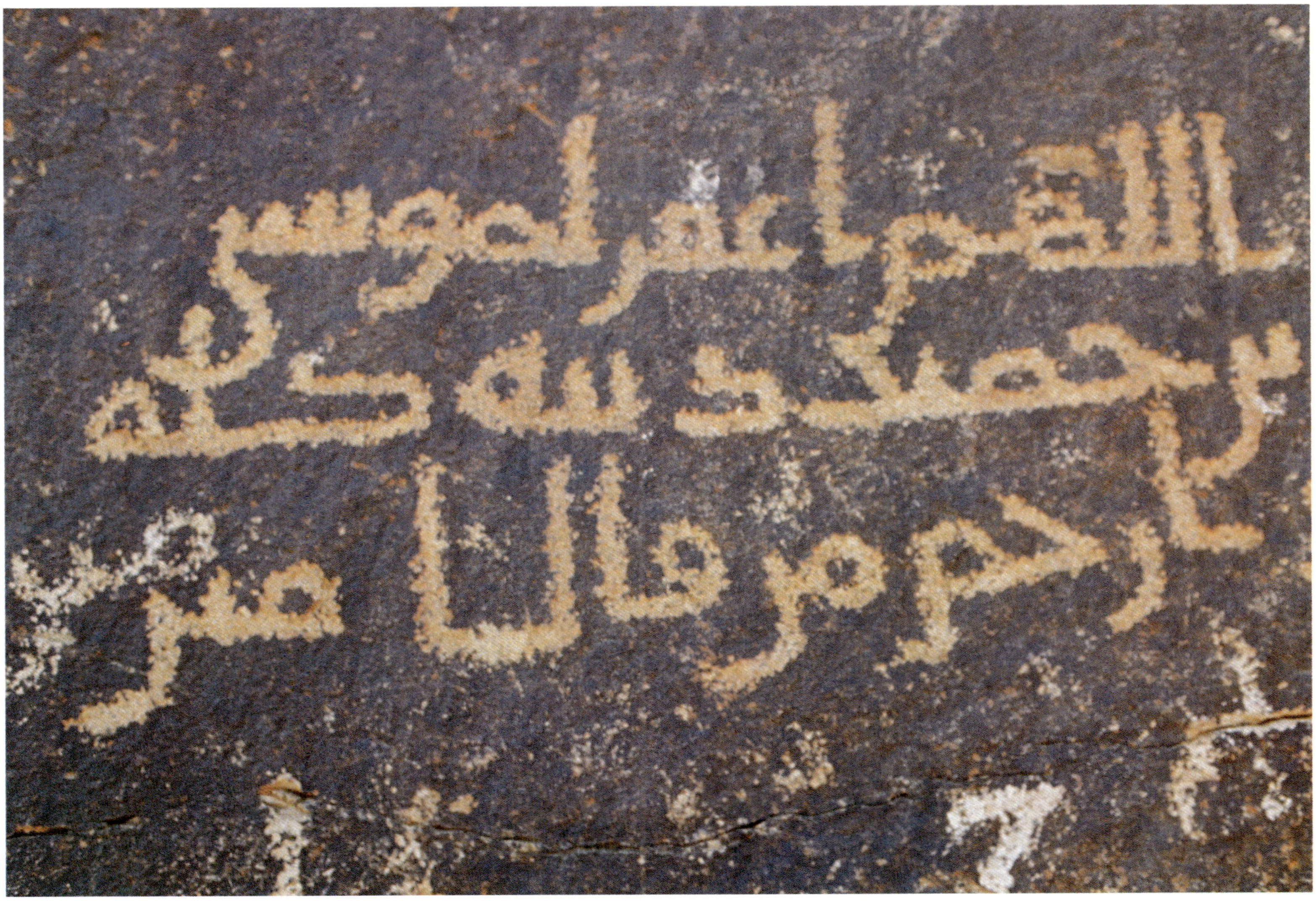

The Heritage of The Kingdom of Saudi Arabia

ANCIENT ROUTES

Left: *Train station along the old Hijaz Railroad. North of Madain Saleh.*
Right: *Commemorative panel with the name "Madain Saleh" inscribed in Arabic script on the exterior of the main station. The inscription includes the building's completion date of 1325 A.H. (1907 A.D.).*
Below: *Remains of Hijaz Railroad cars. Madain Saleh.*
Following overleaf: *Old maintenance hangar and locomotive pit. Madain Saleh.*

In 1900, the Ottoman Sultan Abdulhamid decided to upgrade the Turkey-Madinah Hajj route by building the Hijaz Railroad between Damascus and Madinah. By the time the project was launched, 750,000 Ottoman gold pounds were collected from Muslims worldwide. The building of the 800-mile track took eight years. The completed Hijaz Railroad allowed pilgrims to cross the distance in four days. During World War I, the British officer T.E. Lawrence led a contingent of Arab forces against the Ottomans. They blew up the railroad at several sites to cut the supply route to the Ottoman army. The historic railroad track has not been in operation since.

Nature

Left: *Sunrise over the Sarawat mountain range.*
West of the city of Abha.
The Sarawat chain gradually rises parallel to the Red Sea and separates the central Najd plateau from the Tihamah coastal strip. Some of the Sarawat's peaks reach as high as 7,500 to 9,000 feet above sea level.

NATURE

THE ARABIAN PENINSULA

The Arabian Peninsula is the third largest peninsula in southwestern Asia. It is surrounded by the Sea of Oman and the Arabian Gulf in the east, the Indian Ocean in the south, and the Red Sea in the west. Its northern border, at Sinai, is not naturally defined by a mountain or a river. In fact, Sinai and parts of Iraq and greater Syria are frequently considered part of the Arabian Peninsula.

In the second century, Greek and Roman geographers divided the Arabian Peninsula into three sections called the Arabian Rocky Lands, the Arabian Happy Lands, and the Arabian Sandy Lands. The first included the Sinai Peninsula and the lands that lie southwest of the Syrian desert. Because of the area's rocky plains, it was named *Arabia Petrix* (Rocky Arabia) by the Alexandrian geographer Ptolemy (138-165). The second section covered Yemen and the southwestern edge of the Arabian Peninsula and was called the Green Lands, or *Arabia Felix* (Happy Arabia), in reference to its lush mountains and fertile valleys. The third division, *Arabia Deserta* (Sandy Arabia), covered the remaining parts of the Peninsula.

THE KINGDOM OF SAUDI ARABIA

The Arabian Peninsula covers approximately 1,200,000 square miles, of which the Kingdom of Saudi Arabia occupies around 900,000 square miles. On the basis of its varying topographic and climatic conditions, the Kingdom of Saudi Arabia can be divided, from east to west, into four geographic regions, each with its unique features: al-Hasa, Najd, the Hijaz, and Tihamah.

AL-HASA

Called *Arud* by early Arab geographers, the region of al-Hasa occupies the eastern coast of the Peninsula. It is a sandy strip of land that is no more than a few hundred feet above sea level.

Along most of the coast the sea is shallow and in numerous areas the coastline shifts with the tide. Salt flats (*sabakhat*) are characteristic of the region.

The northern part of the coast consists of uneven sandy plains that support varying densities of bushes and grass. Toward the northwest, the terrain gradually turns into the gravel plains that extend into Iraq.

The southern part of the coast is a sand belt that increases in width as it merges with the dunes of the vast sandy expanse of the Empty Quarter desert. West of the *Rub al-Khali* sands, the dunes turn into a harsh gravelly terrain that extends from al-Hasa beyond the oasis of Yabrin.

West of the sandy coastal strip, the crescent-shaped Summan rocky plateau, eroded by streams that have gone dry, extends from the northern border of the Kingdom to the Empty Quarter.

The region is characterized by a hot and arid climate, with strong seasonal northwest winds that frequently cause major sandstorms.

NAJD

The central plateau, called Najd, extends from the al-Dahna Desert in the east to the Hijaz mountains in the west. Due to the vastness of this region and the diversity of its geography, it is divided into two parts: the highlands are termed *Najd* (the Arabic word for

Tuwaiq escarpment above the al-Dahna Desert. Southwest of the city of Riyadh.

highland) and the lowlands are called *al-Rimal* (the Sands).

Najd proper is considered the heartland of the Kingdom. It is a vast plateau dominated by the al-Ared mountain chain, which extends from the north to the south in a crescent shape. The eastern part of these mountains is called al-Aramah and the western, al-Tuwaiq. The plateau's elevation ranges from low depressions to ridges higher than six thousand feet. From its highest terrain the plateau follows a gentle slope toward the western mountain range of the Hijaz. Najd comprises numerous oases, mountains, and plains as well as many plantations where the best Arabian horses are bred.

The al-Rimal lowlands include large expanses of land, the most notable being the Great Nafud Desert (*al-Nafud*) in the north, the crescent-shaped al-Dahna Desert in the east, and the immensity of the Empty Quarter (*Rub al-Khali*) in the south.

The Great Nafud extends north of Najd toward the Jordanian border. It is a vast sandy depression surrounded by higher plateaux that benefit from scarce seasonal rainfalls. A few waterholes were traditionally used by shepherds and caravans around the edges of the desert. Arid most of the year, the desert nevertheless offers good grazing pastures during its short winter and spring.

Stretching between the Great Nafud to the north, and the Empty Quarter to the south, the al-Dahna Desert is a 750-mile long and narrow sandy crescent. Trapped between two escarpments, it is one of the distinctive formations of the Kingdom.

South of Najd's al-Tuwaiq Mountains, the al-Dahna Desert merges into the Empty Quarter. It is a giant sandy basin, covering approximately 264,000 square miles, that extends from the mountains of Oman in the east to the Yemeni highlands in the west. To the south it is bordered by the coastal mountains of Hadramaut. Mostly uninhabited, it is characterized by torrid temperatures most of the year and below freezing temperatures during part of the winter. Some of its sands are relatively stabilized while others shift according to the prevailing winds.

The continuously changing directions of desert winds form the sands into diverse shapes and designs. For generations, the bedouins were deeply affected by the desert's magnificent vistas and described them in detail in poems and caravan chants (*hudaa*). Explorers and travelers also were fascinated by these breathtaking formations and mentioned them in their writings.

The terrain constituted such an important element in the daily life of the bedouins that every type of sand formation was given a specific name. Thus, *kuthban* describes the common dunes or sand hills formed mainly by the desert wind. *Al-taas*, the cape of a sand dune, generally takes the shape of a horseshoe and ranges from 2 to 150 feet in diameter and from 15 to 150 feet in height. *Al-qaarab* (also called *al-filaq*) is a depression in the ground covered with pebbles and sand in which rain water gathers and grass grows. *Al-khubb*, an easily tractable piece of land, is covered with pebbles through which plants grow and which keep the surrounding sand out. Finally, *al-bahr al-safil* (which means "the sinking sea") is a bed of very fine sand in which objects can sink and disappear. These pools of quicksand exist in places such as al-Ahqaf in the southwestern part of the Empty Quarter. Bedouins know their locations and avoid them.

Relying more on wells than on rainfall, the people of Najd grew various types of grains, citrus fruits, figs, almonds, pomegranates, and palms. Palms were considered the most important trees in the Arabian Peninsula. They provided stems and leaves that were traditionally used as building materials. The trees also generated shade, which promoted the growth of other crops in the soil around them. Their fruit, the date, once constituted an essential ingredient in the daily diet of bedouins as well as city-dwellers. It is said that 172 different grades of dates were grown in Najd.

In earlier times, the Najdis went to great lengths to keep their dates fresh and edible as long as possible. They built special containers, called *jissahs,* made of stone and mud and coated with gypsum. These date storage areas occupied cool, dark areas above the ground, usually in the lower stories of buildings. They were built in the middle of rooms and away from ceilings and walls in order to isolate them from the harsh temperatures outside. The top of the *jissah* was fitted with a wooden or cloth door that allowed access to the dates. The fruit was kept for several months in the *jissah* without drying or spoiling.

Dates earmarked for date molasses were placed in a special *jissah* with a hole at its base. They were covered with palm leaves and heavy rocks, which pressed the dates and caused the syrup to flow through an opening at the bottom of the *jissah*. Date molasses is similar to grape molasses; the only difference is that the former is obtained directly by squeezing, while the latter is made by boiling and thickening grape juice.

The Hijaz

The Arabic word *Hijaz,* meaning barrier or separation, refers to the eastern mountain chain that gradually rises, parallel to the Red Sea coast, from Jordan in the north to Yemen in the south. The chain separates the Najd plateau from the Tihamah coastal region. The Hijaz includes the two holiest cities in Islam, Makkah and Madinah.

The Hijaz is generally divided into two sections by an imaginary line extending between Jeddah and Taif. The area north of this line is considered the Hijaz proper, and that to the south is called *Sarawat* (meaning high peaks). While the Hijaz comprises a mostly rocky and sometimes sandy landscape, it does include a number of lush oases. It is also characterized by several large and inhospitable lava flow areas called *harrat*. The Sarawat region is endowed with fertile soil and is home to some of the oldest settlements.

The Sarawat mountain range receives the largest amount of annual rainfall in the Kingdom. As hot and moisture-laden air currents rise from the Red Sea, they are trapped by the Sarawat's high peaks; forced upward, they collide with the colder air aloft and produce heavy thunderclouds. While the clouds turn into mostly gentle daily afternoon summer rains, the late spring heavy rains can be devastating. Even though much of the rain seeps into the ground, most of it rushes down the steep escarpments with destructive force.

Some of the Sarawat's peaks reach as high as 7,500 to 9,000 feet above sea level, especially at al-Sawdah near the city of Abha. In this mountainous and fertile area, the slopes have been terraced and planted with a variety of grains and trees. The types of trees that grow in the southern Hijaz mountains include evergreen, juniper, cypress, acacia, wild olive, and lotus.

The floral lushness of this area has always attracted a rich and varied wildlife. While some animals have become extinct, many others, such as deer, mountain goats, rabbits, baboons, and a rarely seen number of wolves and leopards, still roam the terrain. The region also supports a wide variety of birds, including Egyptian vultures, falcons, and eagles.

Wheat, barley, and corn are the most important grain crops grown in this part of the Kingdom. They are planted, harvested, gathered, and placed in special silos for future use. In the past, grains assigned for storage were mixed with small amounts of their own soil, for better preservation, then stuffed in special sacks or spread on designated floor areas in dwellings and forts. Grains slated for underground storage were placed into special pear-shaped holes with small openings on top. Each opening was covered with a rock to keep out humidity and to preserve the nutritional value of the grain for long periods of time.

The Hijaz is also noted for its ancient mines, where gold, silver, iron ore, and other metals were once extracted. In 1983 over ten sites were explored in southern Asir. The research yielded tons of slag, remains of smelters, and still explcitable sources of iron, copper, and gold.

Tihamah

Tihamah, which derives from an ancient Sabaean word meaning lowlands, comprises the area between the foot of the Hijaz mountains and the Red Sea coast, from the Gulf of Aqabah in the north to Asir in the south. At certain points, between the mountains and the Red Sea, Tihamah's territory narrows considerably, and at others it widens to as much as 45 miles. Its elevation varies between 1,800 and 2,100 feet above sea level. Tihamah is divided into two general areas: Tihamat al-Hijaz in the north and Tihamat Asir in the south, the former being by far the less fertile of the two.

Tihamat Asir, in turn, is divided into two regions, Tihamat al-Asdar to the east and at the foot of the mountains, and the Coastal Tihamah to the west. Tihamat al-Asdar includes the slopes between the

Al-Tanumah waterfall, Asir. North of the city of Abha.

Sarawat heights and the coastal plain. It enjoys moderate temperatures, low humidity, fertile soil, and an abundance of water. Throughout the ages, cascading waterfalls and small streams have encouraged the inhabitants of al-Asdar to cultivate the mountain slopes and plant grains, fruits, coffee, anacardium, and almonds.

Tihamat al-Asdar is also known for its different varieties of acacia trees, including tamarisk, from which coal was made, and *acacia gummifera,* from which gum Arabic is still extracted. In this area, lotus trees, which can grow up to thirty feet, have wide leaves that can be used as soap. The area also grows *arak,* the evergreen tree from whose roots and branches the popular *miswak* (a small stick, the tip of which is softened by chewing and used for cleaning and polishing teeth) is made.

The Coastal Tihamah includes the plains that lie between the highlands and the Red Sea coast. Although hot and humid, its soil is very fertile because rain water from the mountains, after having lost much of its destructive force, flows down into the valleys carrying with it a rich combination of organic sediments. The farmlands in this area are thus covered with silt, and the soil yields harvests during all four seasons.

The region is known for producing various kinds of herbs and grain, such as corn, pearl millet (*dukhn*), and fava beans, as well as tobacco, indigo, and sesame seeds. The valleys grow reeds, papyrus, and other plants whose branches can be used as roofs for huts built of tree stems.

WATER RESOURCES

Although the climate in the Kingdom of Saudi Arabia differs by region, it is generally characterized by extreme heat accompanied by humidity in the coastal areas and dry heat inland. Places located at a high elevation above sea level enjoy moderate temperatures. While the central desert areas are extremely hot in the midday sun, they become moderate in the morning and at night. The most humid areas of Saudi Arabia are those on the Arabian Gulf and in southern Tihamah.

Rain is a major concern to people in the Kingdom. Traditionally, it has held more immediate significance for the bedouins, who anticipate rainfall and promptly move from pasture to pasture accordingly. Indeed, rainfall generally measures much less than what would be adequate for these lands. Its level varies according to region and time of year. Al-Hasa receives approximately 1.5 to 5 inches of rain annually. While some areas of Najd receive 7 to 12 inches of annual rainfall, most of the region gets only 2.5 to 5 inches. The northern parts of the Hijaz and Tihamah share an annual rainfall of 1.5 to 5 inches; however, southern Hijaz and Tihamah receive an impressive 7 to 24 inches of annual rainfall.

In the mountainous areas of southern Hijaz, rain falls mostly in late summer and autumn. In Najd, however, precipitations occur during December, January, and February. In most areas, rain does not fall continuously for protracted periods of time; but during some years, it is known to have been heavy enough to cover large areas with water and to cause severe floods.

Rainfall in the Hijaz mountains is an important source of water for other parts of the Kingdom of Saudi Arabia. *Wadis* (stream beds that are dry except during the rainy season) are divided into two general categories. The first consists of those streams flowing eastward, such as the wadis of Najran, Bishah, Tathlith, al-Rummah, Hanifah, and al-Dawaser. The second comprises streams flowing westward into the Red Sea, such as the wadis of Damad, Fatimah, Layyah, Wujj, al-Sail, al-Miyah, al-Hamd, al-Hairan, al-Umq, al-Ghar, al-Turayyan, al-Jadayel, and al-Suwar. Even though the majority of eastward streams are lost to the sun's heat and the parched ground, much of the water maintains life in the oases.

An oasis is an area of fertile, arable land that exists either in a mountainous region or in an arid desert region. The Kingdom is endowed with a great number of oases, the most famous of which are al-Jauf and Sakaka in the northern part of the Great Nafud Desert. They are two of the most fertile oases and boast high production levels and adequate water resources. Other notable oases are Taima, at the western edge of the Great Nafud, and Khaibar, which lies about sixty-five miles north of Madinah in an area of hot springs known by the same name. Madinah itself is one of the largest and most fertile oases in the Kingdom. Yanbu al-Nakhl, east of Yanbu al-Bahr, is a cluster of more than ten oases. Other important Hijazi oases include Turabah, al-Kharmah, Raina, and Bishah.

The Najd region also contains many fertile and densely populated oases, among them Shummar, al-Qassim, al-Hasa, al-Qatif, and Yabrin.

Oases are fed by streams that run through canals or waterways into farms and fields, and by underground aquifers whose water is brought up from wells. Some of the ancient wells still provide a fresh and abundant water supply. The depth of wells varies according to the level of underground water and to the type of soil. Ancient wells were either dug in the rock, like those at al-Jiwa springs, or layered with stones, like that at Taima, which is well known for its age and size.

Traditionally, water was drawn up from a well by a mechanism known in Arabic as *al-saniyah* (the water scoop). It consisted of a bar made of palm branches that rested on the edges of two walls erected on either side of the well. The bar was fitted with two wheels and a pair of ropes connected to the sides of a water skin on one end and to an animal on the other. Donkeys or camels were used to pull the ropes. When the animal was closest to the well, the water skin was submerged in the water; as it pulled the ropes away from the well, the water skin was lifted to the mouth of the well and turned over, dumping the water into a canal that irrigated the nearby orchards and farmlands. Wells could be fitted with up to eight such scoops depending on the abundance of water in them and the width of their openings. The number of *saniyahs* was also the measure of a farmer's prosperity.

While there are no lakes in the Kingdom of Saudi Arabia, salt marshes proliferate. Known as *sabakhat*, or salt flats, these are dry lakes which fill up with water after a rainfall. They are like vast plains that contain an enormous quantity of salt. The origin of the *sabakhat* is not known with certainty. It is speculated that they were salt lakes or even residuals of the sea water that covered large expanses of the Peninsula in ancient times.

In the rainy season, a *sabakhah*'s floor becomes very soft and unfit for passage; when it dries up, however, its surface hardens and can be crossed easily by both humans and animals. The hardened soil is covered with a thick layer of salt, which soon breaks up and can be gathered. In some areas, salt was extracted by methods similar to those used in rock quarries. The Kingdom's largest *sabakhat* are generally found on the Arabian Gulf coastline. Others are located near Rabegh, Madinah, Qurayyat al-Milh, and Hadawda in the al-Sirhan Valley.

No active volcanoes are found in the Kingdom today, but there are several that have been calm for many centuries. The most recent record of volcanic activity dates back to the twelfth century, when a volcano near Madinah erupted.

A series of old, inactive volcanoes and cone-shaped elevations can be seen across Arabia. These volcanic elevations are surrounded by expanses of igneous rock called *harrat*. The black color of the rocks in these areas is not, as might be expected, the result of burning in a volcanic eruption. Rather, it is the product of deep oxidation under high temperatures of iron and manganese salts, which are abundant in volcanic rocks.

Water resources in *harrat* areas are not at all scarce. Wells exist in *harrat* and so do streams, but they dry up during the summer. In the midst of the *harrat* there are also plains that turn into pools of water after rainfall; in the spring, these plains become fields of lush, verdant vegetation.

THE HERITAGE OF THE KINGDOM OF SAUDI ARABIA

Right: *Farmer inspecting a date cluster.*
Al-Uyaynah, an oasis 55 miles northwest of the city of Riyadh.
Below: *Palm grove irrigated by a system of well-fed canals.*
Al-Uyaynah.
Opposite: *Clusters of ripening dates.*
Town of al-Hofuf, an oasis 220 miles east of the city of Riyadh.
  Palms were long considered the most important trees in Arabia. They provided stems and leaves that were used as building materials. The trees also generated shade, which promoted the growth of other crops in the soil around them. Their fruit, the date, constituted an essential ingredient in the daily diet of bedouins, as well as city dwellers. It is said that 172 different grades were once grown in Arabia.

NATURE

Left: *Donkeys pulling water skins from a well.*
Town of al-Diriyah, near the city of Riyadh.
Right: *Well and water skins.*
Town of Buraidah, an oasis 320 miles northwest of the city of Riyadh.
Below right: *Camels pulling water from a well.*
Town of Unaizah, an oasis 300 miles northwest of the city of Riyadh.
Below: *Water wheels.*
Al-An valley, near the city of Najran.

In an oasis, irrigation water was traditionally drawn up from a well using water skins and a wheel mechanism called al-saniyah *(the water scoop)*. Wells could be fitted with up to eight such scoops, depending on the abundance of water in them and the width of their opening. The number of saniyahs was also the measure of a farmer's prosperity.
Following overleaf: *Pool of water formed on the desert surface after a heavy, though rare, rainfall.*
Thamamah, 70 miles northwest of the city of Riyadh.

NATURE

Preceding overleaf: *Spring grazing.*
Tuwaiq escarpment, northwest of the city of Riyadh.
  The Kingdom's central plateau, called Najd, extends from the al-Dahna Desert in the east to the Hijaz mountains in the west. The al-Dahna Desert, a 750-mile long and narrow crescent surrounded by higher plateaux, is one of the distinctive formations of the Kingdom. This vast sandy depression, arid most of the year, benefits from scarce seasonal rainfalls and offers lush grazing pastures during its short winter and spring.
Left: *Unhooded by its keeper (saqqar), a hurr falcon is about to take flight.*
Al-Quwayiyah, 100 miles west of the city of Riyadh.
Right: *After catching its prey and relinquishing it to the keeper, the falcon is rewarded with a small tidbit of meat.*
Below: *After the hunt, the bird is once again hooded.*
  Desert falcons and hawks are still domesticated, trained, and prized for their hunting abilities.
  When hunting, a falcon is left hooded until the falconer has the game in sight. Once unhooded, the falcon will quickly spot the prey, swoop toward it, and drop on it with its sharp claws. In the past, some falcons were also trained to hunt gazelles in addition to birds and rabbits. A well-trained falcon will hold the prey and release it only to its keeper. Even a good hawker requires several weeks to train a young bird. While most birds can live up to fifteen years, their first five years are usually considered their best.

99

THE HERITAGE OF THE KINGDOM OF SAUDI ARABIA

Below: *She-camel with its twelve-day-old offspring.*
Al-Mazahimiyah.
Right: *Camel herd roaming at the foot of the Tuwaiq escarpment.*
Al-Mazahimiyah, 30 miles west of the city of Riyadh.

Left: *Arabian oryx.*
Thamamah Wildlife Center, 70 miles northwest of the city of Riyadh.
Right and below: *Zebra, gazelles, and ostriches.*
Thamamah Wildlife Center.

First started in 1962, a major effort is actively underway at the Wildlife Center in Thamamah, and at the National Wildlife Research Center in Taif, to protect and breed a wide range of endangered animal species. Directed by the Saudi National Commission for Wildlife Conservation and Development, the program's aim is to return to the wilderness such animals as zebras, ostriches, gazelles, and other wildlife species that once roamed through the vastness of the Kingdom.

The Heritage of The Kingdom of Saudi Arabia

Right: *Lava rock formations darkened by oxidation. Harrat al-Muwaih, east of the city of Taif.*
Below: *One of the lava flow expanses, called* harrat, *that characterize the Hijaz region. Harrat al-Muwaih.*
Opposite: *After a heavy spring rain, an array of bushes and flowers blooms among volcanic rocks. Harrat Rahat, south of the city of Madinah.*

THE HERITAGE OF THE KINGDOM OF SAUDI ARABIA

NATURE

Left: *Giant dune, approximately 80 feet in height.
Empty Quarter Desert, east of the city of al-Sulayyil.*
Below: *White sand dunes of the Empty Quarter Desert.
East of the city of al-Sulayyil.*
Following overleaf: *Sandstorm over Wadi al-Dawaser.
South of the city of al-Sulayyil.*

Mostly uninhabited, the Empty Quarter Desert covers approximately 264,000 square miles. It is characterized by a torrid climate most of the year and below freezing temperatures during part of the winter.

Opposite: *Yellow Broomrape.*
Al-Dahna Desert, 150 miles south of the city of Riyadh.

Sprouting through the inhospitable sands, this flowery plant springs up for a few weeks between February and March in sandy barren desert spots. The Yellow Broomrape (Cistanche Phelypaea), which can grow up to three feet, is sustained by a deep underground root system that stretches over several yards in search of water. This annual plant produces several thousand seeds which can lie dormant for more than twenty years. They will only germinate after coming in contact with the roots.

Left: *Horned viper.*
Thamamah, 70 miles northwest of the city of Riyadh.

Called a horned viper due to the raised scales above its eyes, this venomous but rarely fatal sand viper is among over 40 species of land snakes found in Arabia.

Below: *After a rare rain, the usually arid sands of the al-Dahna Desert will sprout a blanket of grass and bushes.*
Al-Hunay, 110 miles east of the city of Riyadh.

Following overleaf: *The Great Nafud Desert.*
East of the city of Hail.

The Great Nafud Desert extends north of Najd toward the Jordanian border. It is a vast sandy depression surrounded by higher plateaux. Long regarded as a foreboding barrier, it was cautiously crossed by caravans which followed the historic Darb Zubaidah *that linked the Iraqi city of Kufa to the holy cities of Makkah and Madinah.*

THE HERITAGE OF THE KINGDOM OF SAUDI ARABIA

The Heritage of The Kingdom of Saudi Arabia

NATURE

Preceding left overleaf: *Palm trees.*
Oasis of Taima, 380 miles north of the city of Madinah.
Preceding right overleaf: *Salt flat (*sabakha*).*
Al-Uqair, south of the city of Dammam.
Left: *Camel herd.*
Great Nafud Desert, east of the city of Hail.

   Roaming through the desert, in search of grazing pastures, a herd of camels may wander away for as long as two or three days from the encampment of its bedouin owners.
Below: *Desert vista.*
Great Nafud Desert, east of the city of Hail.

   The continuously changing direction of desert winds forms the sands into diverse shapes and designs. For generations, the bedouins were deeply affected by the desert's magnificent vistas and described them in detail in poems and caravan chants.

117

The Heritage of The Kingdom of Saudi Arabia

Right: *Side and upstream view of the al-Samallaqi dam.*
Twenty miles south of the city of Taif.
Below: *Top of the al-Samallaqi dam.*

Built in pre-Islamic times to control flash floods and store water for irrigation, the dam is approximately 30 feet wide and 600 feet long. It was constructed in successive horizontal sections, according to a technique widely used in southwestern Arabian dams and retaining walls, of large boulders with smaller stones and rock debris tightly packed between them.
Following overleaf: *Mount Shada.*
Near the town of al-Makhwah.

Nature

The Heritage of The Kingdom of Saudi Arabia

Preceding overleaf: *Valley of al-An.*
Najran, 850 miles southwest of the city of Riyadh.
   A lush oasis located on the western edge of the Empty Quarter Desert, Najran was an important caravan center and a first-millennium A.D. Christian city.
Right: *Arabian horse.*
Dirab Arabian horse center, near the city of Riyadh.
Below: *Arabian horses bred in Najran.*
   Even though horses appear in ancient rock inscriptions, it is speculated that the Arabians are a result of a crossbreed of horses that developed in the early stages of the Islamic Empire. After sharing in the early rise of the Empire, Arabia was left in a relative isolation that nurtured the preservation and improvement of the breed.

Arabian horses played a pivotal role in the military history of the world. Regional interest in the horses waned after World War I, however. Since the early 1970s, a breeding and recording program originally initiated by the late King Faisal is now actively encouraging the breeding of true Arabians, and is on its way to reestablishing the Kingdom as their homeland. Under a directive from King Fahd, national races are now strictly limited to pure Arabians.

NATURE

The Heritage of The Kingdom of Saudi Arabia

Right: *For generations, oxen fitted with wooden yokes and plows were used in terrace farming.*
Town of al-Nimas, 140 miles north of the city of Abha.
Below: *In springtime, the terraced highlands and slopes of the southwest yield a rich harvest of wheat and barley.*
Sarawat highlands, west of the city of Abha.

Above: *Shepherdess and her flock.*
Village of al-Masqi, southwest of the city of Abha.
Left: *Young shepherd.*
Al-Sawdah mountain, west of the city of Abha.
Following overleaf: *Goat herd at sunset.*
Sarawat highlands.

    This fertile and mountainous area is characterized by a lush flora that includes forests of juniper, cypress, acacia, and wild olive trees. Prior to the creation of the Asir National Park, which spans 180,000 acres, over-grazing denuded certain areas and threatened the highlands' ecological balance. Since then, controlled grazing and the banning of tree felling have reversed the deforestation trend.

NATURE

Opposite: *Daisy field.*
Jabal Salb, west of the city of Abha.
Above left: *Mountain hurr* (shahin jabali).
Al-Faisal Falcon Center, al-Sawdah Highlands, Asir National Park.

Built in the highlands of Asir, the center is dedicated to the breeding of falcons and to their controlled return to the wild.
Above: *Blue lizard.*
Asir National Park.
Left: *Wild mountain baboons.*
Asir National Park.

The diverse geography of Asir always attracted a rich and varied wildlife. While some animals have become extinct, many others, such as deer, mountain goats, rabbits, baboons, as well as rarely seen wolves, lynxes, striped hyenas, and leopards, still roam the region. With its diversified climate and lush flora, the Asir National Park offers a haven for a wide range of endangered animal species.

NATURE

Left: *Frankincense tree at sunset.
Tihamat al-Asdar, west of the city of Bil-Jurshi.*
Above: *Hardened frankincense tree resin.
Tihamat al-Asdar.*

The resin of the frankincense tree is one of a number of natural aromatic substances that, when burned, give off a pungent scent. In ancient times, frankincense was vital to the rituals of the people of the Middle East and the larger Mediterranean region.

The work involved in collecting the resin usually began in winter by shaving bark strips from the tree trunk. In the spring, the frankincense resin would ooze out and harden into crystals. In the summer, the dried resin was then scraped off the tree or collected from the ground.

The Heritage of The Kingdom of Saudi Arabia

Left: *Called* sabr, *this dracaena grows on rocky elevations.*
Asir Highlands.
Right: *Called* sharfat, *this bush grows on semi-rocky plateaux. It appears almost dead during the dry season but blooms within days after a rain.*
Asir Highlands.
Below right: *Mountain flowers called athrab.*
Jabal al-Hasher, Jizan.
Below: *Korr in bloom (*aloe tomentosa*).*
Jabal Dorum, Asir.

Found on high-altitude rocky slopes, this aloe is also encountered in orange and red. The plant's succulent leaves contain natural antibiotics and are said to have healing properties.

The cool and wet weather of the highlands and the warmer climate of the valleys play host to a wide range of Mediterranean and African plants. While mimosa stands and almond, fig, apricot, and jujube trees are visible in the valleys, honeysuckle and sumac bushes, as well as pistachio trees, prefer the dryer weather of the hillsides.

High above the valleys, forests of juniper and wild olive trees share the highlands with a rich variety of flowers and bushes.

Following overleaf: *Aqabat Man.*
Tihamat al-Asdar, 70 miles southwest of the city of Abha.

In Asir, the word aqabat is used to describe steep passes and wadis that run in a westerly fashion toward the Red Sea coast. Even though much of the highlands rain seeps into the ground, most of it rushes down the wadis and, in some places, forms short streams that support pockets of lush coastal vegetation.

The Heritage of The Kingdom of Saudi Arabia

Preceding overleaf: *Mountain top village in late winter.*
Qubbah, east of the city of Jizan.
   Located to the south of Asir, the region of Jizan shares many of Asir's geographical attributes.
Left: *Jabal al-Hasher in early spring.*
Village of al-Janibah, northeast of the city of Jizan.
Below: *Wadi Qiyar in early spring.*
East of the city of Jizan.
Following overleaf: *Jabal al-Hasher in late spring.*
Northeast of the city of Jizan.

THE HERITAGE OF THE KINGDOM OF SAUDI ARABIA

Left: *Cactus (Euphorbia Genus) in bloom.*
Jabal Faifa, east of the city of Jizan.
  This aloe can grow to over six feet in height and is most often found in clumps.
Below: *Terraced slopes.*
Jabal Faifa, east of the city of Jizan.
Right: *Wadi Qiyar in early spring.*
Bani Malek, east of the city of Jizan.
  Benefiting from a fertile soil, and an impressive 7 to 24 inches of annual rainfall, the century-old terraced slopes of the southwest yield a rich harvest of wheat and barley.

THE HERITAGE OF THE KINGDOM OF SAUDI ARABIA

Right: *Salt flat.*
Farasan Islands, southwest of the city of Jizan.
Below: *Salt flats and eroded rock formations.*
Farasan Islands.

The Farasan Islands are one of the Kingdom's wildlife preservation areas. Despite their hot and humid climate and a harsh environment primarily composed of sandy expanses, low volcanic rock hills, and salt marshes, the islands have become a haven for a large number of endangered species.

The Heritage of The Kingdom of Saudi Arabia

Right: *Harvested sesame stems.*
Coastal Tihamah, city of Jizan.
Below: *Farmer winnowing sesame seeds.*
Coastal Tihamah.
Below right: *Camel-powered press used to crush and extract oil from sesame seeds.*
Town of Sabya, Coastal Tihamah, north of the city of Jizan.
Right: *Ruppel's weaver* (al-nassaj).
Coastal Tihamah.

Millions of birds pass over or through the Kingdom, twice a year, in their migration between Africa and Central Asia. However, only some 300 species are indigenous to the area. While the fertile coastal strip of the southwest is the home of al-nassaj, the cooler altitudes of the highlands are inhabited by hurr falcons, Egyptian vultures, and grackles.

THE HERITAGE OF THE KINGDOM OF SAUDI ARABIA

Right: *Blooming* stabar *shrub.*
Jabal Faifa, Jizan highlands.
   Known as Lavandula Dentata, *this is one of the most common shrubs found in this area. Unlike the garden lavender, the* stabar *does not have a noticeable scent.*
Below: *Wild spring flowers.*
Al-Sawdah highlands, Asir.

Left: *Blooming* adanah *tree.*
West of the city of al-Baha.

Also called elephant tree, this small tree (Adenium Arabicum) grows on medium altitude rocky terrain. Its pink flowers are usually in bloom before the deciduous leaves appear.

Below: *Adanah flower.*
Following overleaf: *Wadi Hali overlook.*
Al-Sawdah highlands, west of the city of Abha.

Reaching as high as 9,000 feet above sea level, the Sarawat mountain range receives the largest amount of annual rainfall in the Kingdom. As hot and moisture-laden air currents rise from the Red Sea, they are trapped by the high peaks; forced upward, they collide with the colder air aloft and produce daily gentle afternoon summer rains and heavy late spring rains that can turn into devastating flash floods.

Architecture

Left: *Qasr Salwa and the Treasury buildings.
Al-Diriyah, west of the city of Riyadh.*
Following overleaf: *Shanana Tower, built in the early 1700s.
Town of al-Rass, 40 miles west of the city of Unaizah.*

Architecture

Architectural Overview

To this date, only a few discovered vestiges truly speak of the architectural styles that were prevalent in the Arabian Peninsula prior to the advent of Islam. It is evident that, at that time, the architectural tradition of the southwestern region of the Peninsula incorporated structural elements and decorative motifs that were distinctly Egyptian in character. On the other hand, the northwestern Nabatean ruins of Madain Saleh have an architectural style that represents a unique synthesis of indigenous creativity with Egyptian and Greco-Roman influences.

Impressive as they are, the ruins of such sites as Qaryat al-Fau, the ancient capital of the Kinda dynasty, or those of Rajajil, a 2000 B.C. settlement near Sakaka, or the vast neo-Babylonian ruins and city walls of Taima offer us only a glimpse of the rich pre-Islamic architectural legacy that remains to be discovered.

Islamic Architecture

Although largely simple and austere, Muslim life during the time of the Prophet Muhammad and the orthodox caliphates had its difficult periods. The ultimate concern of the people was *jihad,* or the struggle to expand the reach of Islam. Consequently, they paid little attention to most other affairs, including architecture and the fine arts.

Architecture during the early years of Islam was functional and unsophisticated. Makkah, for example, contained very few large buildings. Houses of the well-to-do were made of stone; the rest were built with unbaked mud brick. Most were one-story buildings, usually built around a courtyard and a well.

The expansion of the Islamic Empire and the exposure to other peoples and cultures stimulated the Muslims to develop their own artistic potential. As Islam spread to more countries, many craftsmen and builders flocked to Makkah and Madinah, the centers of the new Islamic civilization.

The mosque of Madinah, built by the Prophet Muhammad, became the prototype of Islamic mosques for years to come. Pilgrims who visited the holy places in Makkah and Madinah took back to their countries the fundamentals of mosque-building; soon, mosques proliferated throughout the Islamic world.

After the Arabian Muslims came in contact with other cultures, they started to adapt the newly discovered art forms and architectural styles to their own tastes, life styles, climate, and environment. They introduced columns, arches, vaults, and colonnades and decorated facades of mosques and other buildings. With time, the Muslims developed beautiful and innovative forms, as well as decorative inscriptions, that were in harmony with their religious principles.

When Muawiyah bin Abi Sufian took over the caliphate in the seventh century, he moved the capital of the Islamic caliphate to Damascus. The city's location, close to the borders of the Byzantine Empire, had a great impact on the development of Islamic architecture. The al-Aqsa Mosque in Jerusalem, built by the Umayyads, is a remarkable edifice that symbolizes the Muslims' swift integration of varied architectural forms. Another masterful structure of the Umayyad period is the al-Jami Mosque in Damascus, better known today as the Umayyad Mosque (*Jami al-Amawi*). The Umayyads also constructed a host of buildings and palaces in their cities. Some of their architectural jewels, such as Jordan's eighth-century *Quseir Amra* and Syria's *Qasr al-Hayr al-Sharqi*, can also be found in some remote desert areas.

The Abbassids seized the caliphate in the eighth century and moved its capital to Baghdad, where Persian influences on Islamic art prevailed. This was accompanied by a trend among caliphs, princes, ministers, and the affluent class to build increasingly ornate villas, palaces, and gardens.

The decorative art forms most developed during the Umayyad and Abbassid periods were inscription and ornamentation, especially those associated with Arabic calligraphy. Quranic verses, poetry, and famous sayings were inscribed on walls, cornices, door and window lintels, and decorated in beautiful colors. Building exteriors and floors also were covered with innovative geometric inscriptions.

At the same time, the Abbassids demonstrated a strong interest in constructing major irrigation projects, such as water storage tanks and canals that carried water into basins and pools inside the cities. These were surrounded by lush, resplendent gardens and orchards that contained a multitude of flowers and ornamental plants, as well as a large variety of fruit-bearing trees. The waterworks also extended to the rural areas, where water usage was highly regulated; regional decrees and community accords established the modalities through which water was distributed and used. The projects also included intricate water systems along the main Hajj and trade routes. At each rest station, an elaborate system of dams, canals, underground cisterns, open air pools, and deep wells was developed to capture water after rainfalls and store it for caravans.

Architectural Types

The people of the Arabian Peninsula were divided roughly into two demographic groups: the bedouin nomadic tribes and the settled population. Cattle, goats, sheep, and camels, in particular, were the mainstay of bedouin life; the sale of products derived from livestock satisfied a variety of the bedouins' needs. Although some used caves for shelter, most bedouins lived in tents.

The Tent

Bedouin life has undergone little change throughout the ages. Customs and traditions continue to play an important role in maintaining the tribes' unity and cohesiveness. The basic social unit of bedouins, the tribe, comprises a pyramidal hierarchy based on lineage. The highest and second highest steps in the pyramid denote paternal or other blood lineage, and the remaining represent different degrees of tribal standing. The tribe's cohesiveness serves to protect its members, their wealth, and their common interests, especially water and grain resources.

The tribe is not merely a social structure. It is a whole way of life attesting to man's ability to adapt to his environment. Despite the rapid and profound changes that development and modern technology have brought to Arabia, the bedouin community still plays a vital social as well as economic role there. In addition to providing an ample supply of fresh meats, the bedouins bestow an economic value on arid regions by using them as grazing grounds.

Many bedouins today still inhabit the same valleys, plains, and deserts as their ancestors. Tents remain the bedouins' favorite shelter. Easy to dismantle, carry, and reassemble, they are made of camel and goat's hair, usually woven by family members. Erected in small encampments, each tent belongs to one extended family or clan. The tent is divided into separate quarters, the most prominent of which is *al-raffah*, or the guests' area, where traditional coffee utensils are kept and guests are entertained. The second quarter, called *al-thullah*, or the living quarter, is where family members stay and mats, carpets, and miscellaneous supplies are kept. The third quarter, *al-kusur*, is the cooking area. Each of these sections is separated from the others by a *riwaq*, a woven curtain.

In addition to providing shelter, the tent is a symbol of the bedouins' independent and transient life style and their unending struggle with nature. The openness of the tent signifies the bedouins' generosity.

Settled communities have also existed in Arabia since ancient times, and bedouins and their settled compatriots have maintained interdependent relations throughout the ages. The settled population has lived in cities and towns, engaged in agriculture, industry, and commerce, and traveled to other lands in pursuit of economic prosperity.

The Mosques

The mosque was the first architectural design implemented by the emerging Islamic culture of the Arabian Peninsula. Muslims usually built their mosques in the middle of their communities or adjacent to the markets; thus, worshipers who performed prayers five times a day had easy access to them. Mosques also were found at the gates of cities and towns, and at rest stops along caravan routes.

A typical mosque is comprised of a courtyard and a sanctuary designated for prayer. Inside the sanctuary is the *mihrab*, or prayer niche, which is usually a recess in the mosque indicating the *qiblah*, the direction of prayer facing the Kaabah in Makkah. A major feature of Arabian mosques is the curved or rectangular projection that appears on the outside of the *qiblah* wall. Another characteristic is the usually adjoining built-in *minbar*, the elevated structure from which the Friday sermon (*khutbah*) is delivered. The courtyard is also used for prayers when the mosque overflows with worshipers.

Typically, roofs of old mosques, made of palm stems and branches, were level and had no domes—following the model of the first mosque that Prophet Muhammad built in Madinah in 623. The roof usually rested on wood columns, as well as on stone and mud piers that directly supported the roof structure. At night, mosques were illuminated by clay or stone lanterns fueled by sesame oil or animal fat. They were positioned in little holes or recesses built in the mosque's columns and walls. In the hotter regions, evening and night prayers were sometimes held on the flat rooftops of mosques, which were accessible by open-air staircases built on one of the sanctuary's sides.

One important addition to the original mosque design was the minaret, a cylindrical or tetragonal structure that rises above the other parts of the mosque. It is used as a platform for the call to prayer by the *muezzin*. Even with the widespread use of minarets, some smaller mosques maintained the early tradition of having a set of built-in steps simply leading to the roof, from which the *muezzin* made his call. It is speculated that the tetragonal minaret shapes were influenced by Byzantine architecture, and that the circular shapes derived from Persian architecture. However, another school of thought maintains that both architectural shapes may have evolved in southern Arabia prior to the advent of Islam.

Sanitary facilities, including rows of water taps for ablution before prayer, were usually located near the entrance of the courtyard. To fulfill the requirement of ablution, earlier mosques were built around a well or were provided with cisterns in which rain water was gathered.

In addition to being a place of prayer, the mosque was a gathering place for the community and a center for education. Classes were held under the colonnade surrounding the courtyard; larger communities had a separate school building (*madrasah*) usually connected to the mosque. Students were taught reading and writing and received instruction in the holy Quran, the Hadith (sayings of the Prophet), and other subjects pertaining to religion.

Like other buildings, mosques incorporated varied architectural influences and were constructed with different building materials, depending on the region. In Najd, for example, they had mud walls, while in the Hijaz and Asir, mosques were built mostly with stone then covered with plaster. The walls and doors of some mosques were decorated with ornaments and carved inscriptions. The size of each mosque depended on its location and the density of its surrounding population.

The Quba Mosque. On his way from Makkah to Madinah in 622, Prophet Muhammad stopped at the town of Quba near Madinah and stayed there for about two weeks, during which he built Islam's first mosque: the Quba Mosque. It is said that Muhammad himself participated in the construction with his followers. During his stay in Madinah, Muhammad regularly visited the Quba Mosque and led the people in prayers. To this day, the mosque still retains a special place in the hearts of Muslims.

The Quba Mosque was expanded, in 684, during the rule of the Umayyad caliph Abdulmalek bin Marwan. When Omar bin Abdulaziz, governor of

Makkah and Madinah, rebuilt the Prophet's Mosque in Madinah in 706 on orders from his cousin, Caliph Walid bin Abdulmalek, he also renovated the Quba Mosque, enlarged it, and rebuilt most of its sections with stone and plaster.

The Quba Mosque was renovated again in 1160 during the rule of Jamaleldin al-Asfahani, and then several more times during Ottoman rule. The last renovation was undertaken during the reign of the Ottoman sultan Mahmud II and his son, Sultan Abdulmajid. The date of completion of this last renovation, 1829, still appears carved on a stone plate above the mosque's entrance.

The cornerstone for the most recent renovation of Islam's oldest mosque was laid by King Fahd bin Abdulaziz on 1 December 1984.

THE GRAND MOSQUE OF MAKKAH. The site of the Grand Mosque of Makkah was effectively determined when the Quran instructed Muslims to make the Kaabah (*al-Beit al-Haram*) and the Shrine of Abraham (*Maqam Ibrahim*) a place of worship.

The Kaabah is a simply built cubic stone structure, approximately forty-five feet high and thirty feet wide, that stands in the middle of the Grand Mosque. The Kaabah's southeastern corner includes the Black Stone (*al-Hajjar al-Aswad*). According to tradition, Abraham received the Black Stone from the Angel Gabriel. Each year, the Kaabah's exterior is draped with a new black silk cloth adorned with gold-embroidered verses of the Quran. It is toward the Kaabah that Muslims, the world over, orient themselves for prayer five times a day.

The *Maqam* is a small building near the Kaabah that houses a stone with Abraham's footprints. Today, the fully renovated and greatly expanded Grand Mosque is a huge complex that includes the Kaabah, the *Maqam*, and related places of worship.

Islamic scholars have established that the *Maqam* has remained at the same location since the time of Abraham—through pre-Islamic and Islamic periods up to the present day. But because it is located in a land depression, the *Maqam* was damaged repeatedly by a series of floods. The first documented flood and almost total destruction took place in 638 during the rule of the caliph Omar ibn al-Khattab, who restored the shrine to its original form. The *Maqam* was rebuilt or repaired several times since then.

In the early days of Islam, the Grand Mosque of Makkah was a very simple structure made of raw mud bricks with no surrounding wall. The caliph Omar ibn al-Khattab bought the homes that surrounded it, leveled and replaced them with a courtyard, and constructed a low wall around the mosque in 638. Othman bin Affan, who succeeded Omar as caliph, built the mosque's first colonnades in 646. More improvements were made during the reign of the Umayyad caliph al-Walid bin Abdulmalek. The Grand Mosque was expanded between 754 and 757 under Abu Jaafar al-Mansur, the second Abbassid caliph.

The Grand Mosque sustained a series of repairs, improvements, and expansions over the centuries. One important renovation, ordered by Sultan Salim II, was implemented between 1572 and 1576 by Sinan Pasha, the Ottoman governor of Egypt, who replaced the wooden roof of the mosque with masonry domes. In recent times, one of the most important improvements was undertaken during the rule of King Abdulaziz Al Saud. It included the expansion of the existing colonnades, minarets, courtyards, and other facilities. Such efforts have remained a high priority under Abdulaziz's sons.

With the ever-increasing number of pilgrims to Makkah, the Custodian of the Two Holy Mosques, King Fahd bin Abdulaziz, initiated a set of major improvements that were needed to maintain properly and further expand the Grand Mosque.

THE PROPHET'S MOSQUE IN MADINAH. When Prophet Muhammad moved to Madinah after his brief stay at Quba, he built another mosque where, later, he would be buried. According to tradition, the mosque was part of the Prophet's home and was built where his camel rested after entering Madinah. As with the Quba Mosque, Muhammad personally participated in building the new place of worship, which was later named after him.

The materials used in the construction were unfired mud brick for the walls, palm trunks for columns, and palm leaves and branches for the roof. Initially, the mosque was a very low structure of no more than seven feet high. Its first *qiblah* (the altar indicating the direction of prayer) was located in the north end facing Jerusalem. The *qiblah* remained in that position for seventeen months before it was moved, in compliance with Quranic revelation, so that worshipers would face toward Makkah during prayer. Around the Prophet's Mosque, homes were built (also of brick and palm) to house the early Muslims who accompanied Muhammad from Makkah. After the battle of Khaibar in the seventh year of the Hijrah, Muhammad ordered the mosque expanded in order to accommodate the increased number of converts to Islam. During this first renovation its rectangular plan was made a perfect square.

Omar ibn al-Khattab wholly renovated and expanded the Prophet's Mosque in 638. It was reconstructed using stone and plaster, the columns replaced with carved stones reinforced with steel pellets and melted lead, and the roof rebuilt with teak wood. Additional facilities were added by Caliph Othman bin Affan during 649-650.

Several decades later, al-Walid bin Abdulmalek, the Umayyad caliph, entrusted Omar bin Abdulaziz, the governor of Madinah, with adding new courtyards and other facilities to the mosque. Omar hired Byzantine and Egyptian builders to rebuild the mosque in stone. This important renovation work was implemented between 706 and 709. The Abbassid caliph al-Mahdi added more facilities to the mosque during the years 777-781.

In 1256 the Prophet's Mosque and surrounding buildings were burned down in a fire caused by one of the mosque's lamps. The only part that was spared was a domed structure, containing the mosque's valuables, which had been built in the courtyard in 1180 by one of the Abbassid caliphs. The following year, the Abbassid caliph al-Mustasim initiated the repairs later completed by the sultan of Egypt, al-Zahir Baybars al-Bunduqdari

Over the years, the increased influence of the Mamluk rulers of Egypt led to a series of other repair and improvement projects. In 1474, King al-Ashraf Qait Bay ordered a major renovation of the mosque's roofs, columns, walls, and minarets. The work included the construction in 1476 of a stone dome over the Prophet's tomb.

After the Ottomans seized the Islamic caliphate, they also assumed the responsibility of looking after the Prophet's Mosque. In 1817 Sultan Mahmud built the grand dome of the mosque and had it painted green, the color it remains to this day. One of the major restorations and expansions, however, was implemented by Sultan Abdulmajid between 1848 and 1860. As part of the renovation work, the well-known calligrapher Abdallah Zuhdi was sent from Constantinople to Madinah, where he spent three years adorning the mosque's domes and walls with Arabic inscriptions. These included Quranic verses, poetry, and the numerous names and titles of the Prophet.

The first modern expansion in this century was initiated by King Abdulaziz Al Saud and continued by his heirs. Recently, the Custodian of the Two Holy Mosques, King Fahd bin Abdulaziz, initiated a comprehensive program of improvements of the Prophet's Mosque in Madinah.

REGIONAL ARCHITECTURAL TYPES

The major architectural types in the Kingdom of Saudi Arabia have their roots in the traditions of the country's main regions: al-Hasa, Najd, the Hijaz, and Tihamah.

AL-HASA. The old townships of Saudi Arabia's Eastern Province, al-Hasa, lie between the coast of the Arabian Gulf in the east and the desert in the west. The climate there is very hot and humid throughout most of the year and more prone to extremes than the temperature and weather conditions of the cities on the Red Sea coast.

Old buildings and houses in the Eastern Province are constructed of limestone, a rock found on the coast and inland, and with tree trunks fitted between buttresses to connect the buildings' components. Outer walls are coated with plaster or gypsum and the roofs composed of branches and stems of palms or other trees. Although the structures do not conform to one specific form, a common pattern unites them, one characterized by attractive proportions and orderly plaster ornamentation.

The roof structures of some older buildings include ventilation towers equipped with openings which draw air into a duct system that reaches inner hallways and rooms, thus helping to moderate temperatures inside.

The buildings in the Qutaif region are of various heights. The lower structures are usually fitted with small windows, while the taller ones have wide circular or oval windows that facilitate air flow into the rooms. Some of the older roofs incorporate small rooms with wide windows that rise one or more stories. Called *tayyarahs*, these rooms are airy and comfortable on hot summer nights. Similar roof structures are found, in the Hijaz, in the old buildings of Jeddah.

Over the centuries, the inhabitants of the Arabian Gulf area carefully considered seasonal variations in the direction of wind as they planned their buildings. Accordingly, ventilation apertures always were designed to face the wind directions prevalent in the region.

NAJD. In Najd, as in other regions, architectural types and composition, including structure, style, size, and number of stories, generally vary according to the needs and status of the owners. Buildings were typically constructed with either unfired mud brick or mud walls. This building material was widely used because of its load-resistance characteristics, and its important quality as a good heat insulator. In addition, it was abundant, inexpensive, and easy to use.

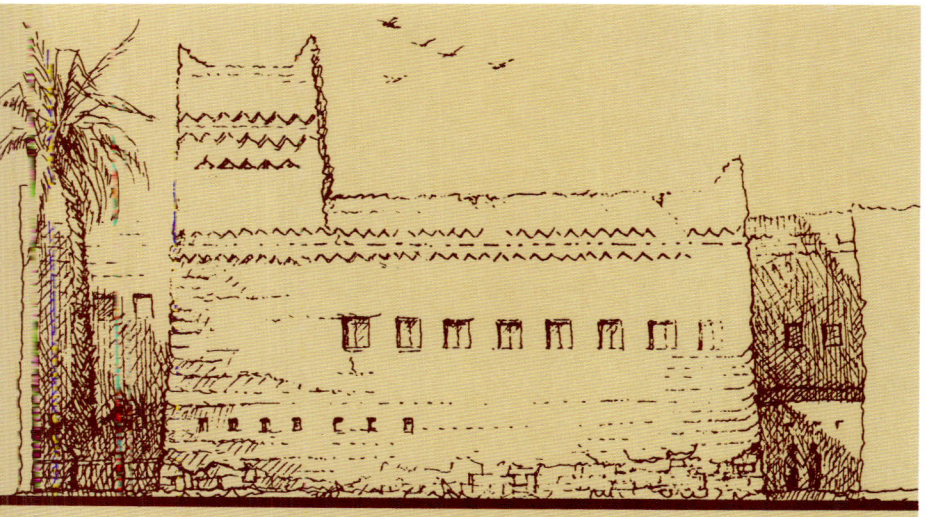
Al-Tajul traditional house, built around 1863, town of Unaizah, Najd.

Unfired mud brick was made of soil or silt collected from the valleys after the rain water dries out. After it was brought to the construction site, it was soaked with water and mixed with straw and other fibers. The mixture was then left for a few days to be trodden by livestock to increase its cohesiveness. It was kneaded and turned over until it acquired the right consistency, then cut into small blocks or poured into wood or iron molds and left to dry.

Mud walls were also built without pre-drying the mud (*libin*). In this case, the walls were built in tapered horizontal rows that were slightly elevated at the corners in order to increase their stability. Upon completion of each small portion, the builders would smooth all surfaces with a piece of wood or metal. Walls were made very thick in order to assure structural stability. As a result, they acquired excellent insulation characteristics. Roofs were built with tamarisk or palm tree stems covered with branches and daubed with mud. Flat stones also appear in both roof and floor structures. While restricted in its availability, stone was frequently used in building foundations at a depth of three to six feet below the outer and inner building walls.

In the northern region of Najd, traditional houses comprise rows of rooms that surround an inner courtyard; room doors and windows open into this area—only in rare cases are there portals to the outside. To assure privacy, the larger homes have two entrances: one for men and their male visitors, and the other for women. The *majlis*, a room designated for entertaining guests, is situated on either the ground level or the second floor. In one corner of the *majlis* is the *wujar*, the place where coffee is prepared.

Generally, the main doorway is wide and takes a rectangular or arched shape. The door is made of carved wood and adorned with colored drawings of plants and flowers. The walls of the entrance way are coated with mud and plaster. Examples of these old structures are found in many cities, such as Riyadh, Shaqra, Hail, and Sadus.

Old houses in southern Najd are composed of several stories. The main entrance, on the ground floor, is part of the front of the building and opens into a courtyard comprising fodder storage chambers, animal barns, sheds for agricultural equipment, and the main staircase. The mill and storage areas for grain and foodstuffs occupy the first floor; these have small openings for ventilation that are blocked by dried thorny plants to keep out birds and rodents. The upper floors contain the various family rooms, kitchen, laundry area, bathroom, water storage tank, a private chamber for the family elder, and a terrace surrounded by a high wall. The wall is usually perforated in a decorative fashion to allow for air circulation. During the day the terrace may be used for housework, while at night it becomes the family gathering place.

THE HIJAZ. The similarities of the traditional buildings of northern and central Hijaz, particularly in the cities of Makkah, Madinah, Jeddah, and Taif, are due to the influence of a certain architectural style that was prevalent in Egypt, Syria, and Turkey during the Ottoman era. Most older homes are composed of two to four stories and are entered from an arched doorway. The outer walls are usually plastered with lime left white or colored in very light blue. Doors and windows, inscribed with colorful drawings, are made of wood imported at times from India, Java, and other locations. Doors, windows, and the main facades of some larger buildings are decorated with carved wood screens called *mushrabiyahs*. These ornamentations allow privacy while promoting the flow of fresh air into the house. Jars filled with water were hung behind the wooden screens and kept cool by the flowing air.

In Jeddah and other coastal towns, load-bearing building walls were constructed with limestone reinforced with wooden beams. On the exterior, the houses have *mushrabiyahs* that extend over two or three floors.

Doors comprise doubled, heavy teakwood leaves, decorated with deeply carved ornamentations. They are fitted with heavy hardware and circular knockers made of forged iron.

In contrast with the north, southern Hijaz is characterized by a diversity of architectural styles. This densely populated region is endowed with a moderate climate, abundant forests and water resources, and fertile land. It is one of the richest areas in agriculture as well as natural and human resources, and one of the most prosperous in the entire Kingdom.

From generation to generation, the people of southern Hijaz have adhered to the architectural patterns and designs inherited from their ancestors. Because of the abundance of trees, wood was used extensively in construction. By and large, however, the older buildings were made of stone, which is still found throughout the regions of Ghamed, Zahran, and the province of Asir. In addition to its availability, stone is still appreciated for its durability and resistance to weather changes.

As a result of a history marred by centuries of foreign invasions and regional turmoil, the concern with safety and security prompted the southern Hijazi population to excel in the construction of fortified structures, such as forts (*hosns*) and watchtowers (*qasabahs*), to protect themselves and their resources. While *hosns* served as dwellings, defense posts, and grain storage facilities, *qasabahs* were used only as observation posts for defense purposes. They were built with circular bases and could accommodate only a small number of men, whereas *hosns* were built larger and constructed according to a rectangular plan. *Hosns* and *qasabahs* also were used to communicate with neighboring areas—fires were lit on their rooftops to alert others of an impending danger.

Traditionally, a fort could be owned by an individual or family; it also could serve as the collective property of whole villages and be used mainly as a grain storage facility. In the latter case, separate quarters within the *hosn* were assigned to different groups or families in the village.

Many *hosns* and *qasabahs* combined the advantage of a strategic location with the merit of being functional and aesthetically pleasing. They were usually constructed in the middle of a group of homes, near the gateways of towns, in open plains and valleys, near wells and springs, and, especially, on hills and mountaintops.

In some parts of Asir, building facades were decorated strikingly with white, shiny quartz stones, called *maru*, juxtaposed with the dark stones of the building. Designed with defense needs as a priority, the entrances displayed a wide range of protective accesses. In most cases, the gates were flanked with special openings behind which the guards could lie in wait. Doors were made of tough wood to resist intruders. To protect the wood from insects and the elements, the doors were coated seasonally with a natural resin called *qutran*.

Outer and inner walls were plastered with mud. In some areas, painted designs graced most walls and stairwells; these were created largely by women, many of whom were known in their communities for their skill and artistry. Dyes produced from local plants provided many colors of paint; the natural green, extracted mainly from the clover plant, was favored most.

Mud used in plastering walls and staircases was

Al-Umari traditional house, built around 1844, town of al-Makhwah, Tihamah.

made by a special process. First, soil was collected and cleared of pebbles and other impurities. After it was mixed with a small amount of chopped and crushed straw, water was added gradually until the mixture was moderately soaked. It was then kneaded into a paste and spread promptly over the required area. The mud was smoothed with metal or wood tools until it became a polished, shiny surface. Before it hardened completely, women vigorously rubbed a green dye into the areas designated for decoration. With other colors, they drew different designs into the green background, thus turning an otherwise dull area into a surface bursting with vibrant hues and striking patterns. Some of the better preserved examples of such artwork have survived to this day in a number of homes in Rijal-Alma, a town in the Asir region. Mud also was used in a similar fashion on floors; in this case, the drying mud was not colored but hand-formed into repetitive decorative patterns.

Many older buildings in southern Hijaz are constructed with quarried stones mostly left in their original shapes. Walls built with these stones have a large base and become narrower as they rise from one floor to another, making the structure resemble a truncated pyramid. This unique design yields an attractive and highly stable architectural form. In these multistory structures, staircases conform to the shape of the whole building. They originate from wide bases and narrow gradually as they rise upward until, at the uppermost level of the building, they measure no more than three feet in width.

frame made of branches. Their outer and inner walls were partially coated with mud or plaster. The interior surfaces were decorated with drawings of plants and animals, as well as with hanging plates of different shapes and colors. The design of the huts was usually spherical or oval in shape. Each dwelling hut, called *ushah,* was either isolated or formed part of a small community; the larger huts were used as dwellings while the smaller ones served as storage areas for grain and fodder, and as a shelter for animals.

In the old pearl fisher Island of Farasan, dwellings were built of limestone and adobe. While the buildings' exterior usually remained sober, the interior walls, specially those of the *majlis,* were frequently decorated with elaborately carved gypsum patterns. In this year-round hot and humid climate, the lace-like quality of the carvings promoted the continuous ventilation of the interior spaces. While sharing certain similarities with some of the plaster work found in Najd, the traditional decorative interiors of Farasan are characterized by their own style and proportions.

Al-Majhud traditional house, built around 1853, town of Bil-Jurshi, Hijaz.

TIHAMAH. The northern and central traditional architectural styles of the Red Sea coastal region of Tihamah are similar to those found in the adjoining areas of the Hijaz. In contrast, most of the old dwellings of southern Tihamah are similar in construction to the huts found on the nearby eastern coast of Africa.

The dwellings, fully adapted to the area's prevalent hot and humid weather, were constructed of woven reeds, straw, and doum tree leaves secured to a domed

ORNAMENTATION AND CONSTRUCTION.

White quartz stones, known as *maru,* were used extensively for decorating door and window frames, and building facades in northern and southern Hijaz. Plaster ornamentation also proliferated in Najd as well as in southern Hijaz and Tihamah.

Plaster's many attributes suited the various climate of the regions. In addition to being a good heat insulator, it is highly resistant to rain and hail. Since many buildings were built or coated with mud, seasonal plaster coatings proved an ideal protection against the elements.

Plaster was also utilized for other functional and decorative purposes. Although thick latticework over doorways (to ensure privacy while allowing continuous ventilation) was usually made of wood, intricately carved and hollowed plaster was also used in areas where wood was lacking or where wood carvers were rare. Decorative plaster motifs reflected the designs and forms of the original wooden *mushrabiyahs*. Even their names were similar, referring to trees, plants, flowers, and geometric designs.

From an historical standpoint, however, plaster is not a very durable building material. It could therefore not be found in old ruins, especially those of ancient settlements close to the sea. While it is estimated that plaster survives between fifty to a hundred years in buildings constructed on the coast, its life span increases rapidly as one moves inland.

Until not too long ago, an individual wishing to construct a house or any other building first reached an agreement with a master builder from the surrounding area, who undertook to implement all the work necessary to finish the job. Generally, the master builder possessed extensive experience in planning and executing all aspects of the construction process; he learned his profession simply through practice and without formal instruction or training. He was familiar with the various stone quarries in the region, the types of stone available, and how best to acquire them and transport them to the site. Stones were either quarried or gathered from nearby fields, loaded on donkeys and camels, and moved to the construction site, where they were cut into the required shapes and fastened in place. The builder also knew where and how to obtain the wood needed in the construction work.

Trees usually were cut during the winter while the sap was still in the roots. Trunks and branches were then hauled to designated sites, where the bark was removed and the timber cut to pieces. These were then moved to the construction site, where the requisite doors, windows, and other wooden components were made.

As the building progressed, the master builder would outline each floor, ensuring the correctness of his measurements and the positions of the load-bearing structure. Working with him as apprentices were a select number of skillful and reliable family members. Construction workers were paid on a daily or weekly basis depending on the agreement with the prospective owner. They worked from sunrise to late afternoon; rest periods comprised a morning break in the early hours of the day and another break at noon for lunch and midday prayers. The work day ended prior to the hour of the afternoon prayer.

The traditional wooden measuring stick used in construction is called a *quddah* (also a *dhiraa*, or arm's length) and measures around twenty-four inches. Each *quddah* is divided into eight units known as *qirats*. It would appear that the *quddah* was used mainly in Makkah, Madinah, Taif, and other areas of the western Arabian coast.

ARCHITECTURE

Left: *Restored minaret of the old Palace of al-Diriyah.*
Below: *Restoration of the Palace of al-Diriyah.*

The House of Saud traces its beginning to the middle of the 15th century, when the oasis of al-Diriyah, through a combination of successful farming and strong leadership, grew from a small rural settlement into a politically influential town. In the early 1700s, during the rule of Saud, the son of Muhammad bin Muqrin, al-Diriyah was considered one of the strongest and most important emirates in the Peninsula.

In 1740, Muhammad bin Saud, Saud's son and a devout Muslim, lent all his support to the religious reformist movement of Shaikh Muhammad bin Abdulwahab. As a result, al-Diriyah's influence as the capital of the House of Saud extended over most of the Arabian Peninsula.

In 1811, the Ottoman governor of Egypt, Muhammad Ali Pasha, restored Ottoman rule over the Hijaz and the two holy cities of Makkah and Madinah. Seven years later, the Egyptian and Ottoman armies succeeded in seizing most of Najd. After fierce fighting, al-Diriyah was captured and then razed.

Its ruins stand as a testimony to the House of Saud's early struggle for independence.

Architecture

Left: *Interior Court, old Governor's Palace.*
Town of al-Hofuf, an oasis 220 miles east of the city of Riyadh.
Right: *Roof pavilion, old Governor's Palace.*
Below: *Main staircase, old Governor's Palace.*

  Built around 1907, during the reign of King Abdulaziz, the palace represents a harmonious blend of architectural details and proportions.

Architecture

Opposite: *Qasr al-Masmak.*
City of Riyadh.
Right: *Interior alley, Qasr al-Masmak.*
 The triangular openings in the walls promote continuous ventilation.
Below right: *Interior courtyard and well, Qasr al-Masmak.*
Below: *Portico with wooden roof structure, Qasr al-Masmak.*
 Qasr al-Masmak, a historic fort and palace, was taken over in 1902 by Abdulaziz bin Abdulrahman, who stormed the fortified palace with 40 of his warriors. He made Riyadh the nucleus of an expanding rule that began in the Najd region and then covered the entire area that is now known as the Kingdom of Saudi Arabia.

Left: *Commemorative carved plaster plaque, dated 1358 A.H. (1935 A.D.).*
Qasr al-Muraba, city of Riyadh.
Below: *King Abdulaziz's audience parlor* (majlis), *Qasr al-Muraba.*
Right: *Interior court of Qasr al-Muraba.*
  Built in 1935, the palace was King Abdulaziz's official residence when in Riyadh.

The Heritage of The Kingdom of Saudi Arabia

ARCHITECTURE

Left: *Arched interior prayer hall, Mosque of al-Sudus.*
Village of al-Sudus, 40 miles northwest of the city of Riyadh.
Below left: *Minaret, Mosque of al-Sudus.*

Built as an integral part of the small fortified village of al-Sudus, the mosque is abutted on three sides by the village's closely packed mud houses.

Right: *Interior portico of al-Hazem Mosque.*
Town of al-Majmaah, 160 miles northwest of the city of Riyadh.
Below: *Minaret and roof of al-Hazem Mosque.*

Built in 1787, the mosque's prayer hall has the same mud-brick keel-arches found in neighboring areas.

175

Above: *Arched interior of al-Hilaliyah Mosque, built around 1785.*
Village of al-Hilaliyah, 475 miles northwest of the city of Riyadh.
Right: *Courtyard of al-Hilaliyah Mosque.*

ARCHITECTURE

The Heritage of The Kingdom of Saudi Arabia

Below: *Qasr al-Dawadmi, north facade, built around 1780, during the reign of King Abdulaziz.*
Town of al-Dawadmi, 240 miles west of the city of Riyadh.
Left: *Watchtower and south wall, Qasr al-Dawadmi.*
Right: *Courtyard, house of Abdulrahman al-Sibai, built around 1890.*
City of Shaqra, 130 miles northwest of Riyadh.

ARCHITECTURE

Right and above: *Interior courtyard and upper floor details, house of Sulaiman bin Abdallah al-Bati, built around 1930. City of Buraidah.*
Opposite: *Mosque minaret.*
Town of Uyun al-Jawa, east of the city of Buraidah.
   The tapered minaret structure is characterized by a wide base and by horizontal ridges which protrude over the minaret shaft. The style of the minaret and the crenellations at the top and on the courtyard's (sahn) walls is typical to the region.

Architecture

THE HERITAGE OF THE KINGDOM OF SAUDI ARABIA

Left: *Door and wooden lock detail.*
City of Riyadh.
Right: *Door and lock detail from the home of the late Shaikh Muhammad Abdulwahab.*
Town of al-Huraimala, 80 miles northwest of Riyadh.
Far right: *Exterior door detail.*
City of Buraidah.
Lower far right: *Decorated and reinforced exterior door.*
City of Unaizah.
Below right: *Decorated exterior door.*
City of Unaizah.
Below: *Reinforced exterior door.*
City of Unaizah.
Below left: *Interior door with ventilation openings.*
City of Shaqra.

Most of the old doors in Najd were made from tamarisk wood, adorned with geometric designs and painted with different colors. The doors were frequently reinforced and decorated with large nails. Most lock mechanisms, including latches and keys were also crafted out of wood.

Architecture

Left: *Hand-woven bedouin tent, closed on the side facing the prevailing winds.*
Al-Dahna Desert, west of the city of Riyadh.
Right: *Tent interior.*
Village of Jubbah, at the edge of the Great Nafud Desert, 50 miles northwest of the city of Hail.
   In contrast with its stern exterior, the tent's interior is covered with vivid patterns in hand-woven wool.
Far right: *Al-Sadiq Salem, a bedouin tending his flock.*
Village of Raghabah, 90 miles from the city of Riyadh.
Lower far right: *In each tent, the guest area* (al-raffah) *is where coffee traditionally is offered to guests.*
Near al-Rabadhah, about 130 miles east of the city of Madinah.
Below: *With its sides open, a tent reveals the woven curtains* (riwaqs) *that separate its different interior quarters.*
Village of Jubbah, at the edge of the Great Nafud Desert, 50 miles northwest of the city of Hail.

ARCHITECTURE

The Heritage of The Kingdom of Saudi Arabia

Architecture

Opposite: *King Abdulaziz Garrison.*
City of Hail, 500 miles northwest of the city of Riyadh.
Left: *Watchtower, King Abdulaziz Garrison.*
Below: *Rooftop, King Abdulaziz Garrison.*
Following overleaf: *Zabal Citadel, built around the middle of the 19th century.*
Town of Sakaka, an oasis on the northern edge of the Great Nafud Desert.

Left: *Carved plaster wall details.*
Manfouhah quarter, city of Riyadh.
Below: *Carved plaster wall details*
Town of al-Rass, 40 miles west of the city of Unaizah.
Below left: *Decorated plaster wall remains.*
City of Shaqra, 140 miles west of the city of Riyadh.
Right: *Shanana Tower, built by the al-Khalifah family in the early 1700s.*
Town of al-Rass, 40 miles west of the city of Unaizah.

THE HERITAGE OF THE KINGDOM OF SAUDI ARABIA

Preceding overleaf: *Qasr Marid, also known as Qasr al-Ukaider, an early stone and mud-brick Islamic structure built on top of 300 B.C. foundations.*
Oasis of al-Jauf, 40 miles west of the city of Sakaka.
Above: *Watchtower, built around 1850 in the vicinity of Qasr Marid.*
Oasis of al-Jauf.
Right: *Stone minaret and mosque of Caliph Omar.*
  Standing amidst the oasis and old town of al-Jauf, the mosque structure has witnessed many alterations. Its foundations are attributed to Caliph Omar and date to approximately 640 A.D. Not too long ago, the town's buildings adjoined the four-sided minaret, and one of the streets passed through its arched base.

THE HERITAGE OF THE KINGDOM OF SAUDI ARABIA

ARCHITECTURE

Preceding overleaf: *Qasr Abu-Lawhah.*
Madain Saleh, approximately 200 miles northwest of the city of Madinah.
Left: *Tomb facades carved in the western cliff of Qasr al-Bint.*
Madain Saleh.
Top: *Tomb pediment incorporating Greco-Roman influences. The pediment center is adorned with a Nabatean eagle, and the remains of funerary urns can be seen on either side.*
Madain Saleh.
Above: *Tomb entrance adorned with two sculpted lions holding a rosette.*
Madain Saleh.

The Nabatean ruins of Madain Saleh date to the first century B.C. The rock-carved tombs testify to the fact that Nabatean society must have known an advanced form of civilization.

During Emperor Trajan's reign, the Romans became increasingly concerned with Persia's influence on the eastern shores of Arabia. To counter the Persians' gains, Trajan sought to further Rome's control of the western trade routes of the Peninsula. In 106 A.D., the Romans captured the city of Petra and precipitated the downfall of the Arabian Kingdom of Nabatea.

THE HERITAGE OF THE KINGDOM OF SAUDI ARABIA

Left: *Quran class at the Quba Mosque.
Southwestern edge of the city of Madinah.*
Below and right: *General views of the Quba Mosque.*

During the Prophet's journey to Madinah, in 622, he stayed in Quba for three days prior to entering the city of Madinah. During this short stay, he prayed on the site of the Quba Mosque, which is therefore honored as the first mosque site in Islam.

The latest set of improvements to the mosque were initiated by King Fahd bin Abdulaziz and completed in 1986.

ARCHITECTURE

201

THE HERITAGE OF THE KINGDOM OF SAUDI ARABIA

Above: *The Prophet's Mosque (al-Masjid al-Nabawi) entrance known as Bab al-Salam.*
City of Madinah.
Right: *General view of the Prophet's Mosque expansion program commissioned by the Custodian of the Two Holy Mosques, King Fahd bin Abdulaziz.*

Contemporary improvements of the Prophet's Mosque were first initiated by King Abdulaziz in 1953. In 1975, King Faisal commissioned a second Saudi improvement program that greatly expanded the Mosque and its capacity.

The last improvement program, initiated by King Fahd in 1982, includes an impressive expansion of the Mosque and of its surrounding assembly plazas and related infrastructure. When completed, the prayer areas will approximate 4,000,000 square feet and will accommodate over 650,000 worshipers on a regular basis and as many as 1,000,000 worshipers on special occasions.

Opposite: Historic green dome of the Prophet's Mosque. City of Madinah.
  The present green dome replaces several previous stuctures that were repeatedly destroyed by fire. The dome was last rebuilt in 1818 during the reign of the Ottoman Caliph Mahmud II. The south-east minaret visible behind the dome was built in 1487 by the Mamluk Sultan Qayt Bay.
Right: Detail of the Prophet's Mosque colonnades completed in the late 1970s during the second Saudi improvement program.
Below: Section of the Prophet's Mosque prayer hall and colonnades built in the late 1800s by the Ottomans.

ARCHITECTURE

Preceding overleaf: *Worshipers assembled for evening prayer at the Grand Mosque of Makkah (Al-Masjid al-Haram). City of Makkah.*
Opposite: *Two of the nine 270-foot-tall minarets that adorn the Grand Mosque of Makkah.*
Above: *Part of the major improvements carried out, in 1966, at the Grand Mosque of Makkah.*
Left: *Restored colonnade originally built during the reign of the Ottoman Sultan Mahmud (1571-1576).*

The first contemporary renovation of the Grand Mosque of Makkah was ordered by King Abdulaziz. The work included enlarging the Mosque from approximately 290,000 square feet to over 1,600,000 square feet. Started in 1955, the work was ultimately completed in 1961 during the reign of King Saud.

More recently, a royal decree issued in 1983 by the Custodian of the Two Holy Mosques, King Fahd bin Abdulaziz, spearheaded another impressive improvement program. When completed, the total prayer areas will be in excess of 3,100,000 square feet. The Grand Mosque will then be able to accommodate over 695,000 worshipers on a regular basis and over 1,000,000 worshipers on special occasions.

The Heritage of The Kingdom of Saudi Arabia

Above left: *Grand Mosque of Makkah 270-foot-high minaret.*
Above: *Detail of the architectural motifs that adorn the new exterior walls of the Grand Mosque.*
Left: *The Grand Mosque's covered* Massa *structure stretches several hundred feet between the two small hills where, according to Islamic tradition, Hagar and Abraham's son Ismael were stranded. Crossing the distance between the two hills, pilgrims reenact Hagar's desperate search for water until the Angel Gabriel led her to the Zamzam Well.*
Opposite: *Pilgrims performing the* tawaf, *the ritual circling of the Kaabah.*

   The Kaabah is a simple stone cubic structure that stands at the same place were Abraham and his son Ismael offered prayers and built the original House of God. The Kaabah represents the spiritual center of Islam, and symbolizes the oneness and centrality of God. The first row of low arches surrounding the courtyard were built in the late 1570s by the Ottomans. The second row of taller colonnades were part of the expansion program started, in 1955, by King Abdulaziz.

THE HERITAGE OF THE KINGDOM OF SAUDI ARABIA

212

Architecture

Far left: *The Grand Mosque as seen from Fort Jiyad.*
City of Makkah.
Left: *Unstained wooden mushrabiyah carving detail, dating from the late 1800s.*
City of Makkah.
Right: *Wooden* mushrabiyah, *dating from the late 1800s.*
City of Makkah.
Below right: *The hills surrounding the city of Makkah, as seen from Fort Jiyad.*
Below: *Fort Jiyad.*
  Overlooking the Grand Mosque of Makkah, the fort was built in 1781 by Surour bin Mussaed, the Emir of Makkah.

THE HERITAGE OF THE KINGDOM OF SAUDI ARABIA

Left: Historic houses with wooden mushrabiyahs.
Haret al-Sham, Old Jeddah.
Above: Mushrabiyah *carving detail.*
Haret al-Sham, Old Jeddah.
Right: Nassif House.
Haret al-Sham, Old Jeddah.

The house was built in 1878 by Shaikh Muhammad Hussain Nassif, a Jeddah notable. The builder had its stones quarried from rock formations by the Red Sea and moved on pack animals to the construction site. The sandy grounds were dug down to the rocky bed, on which the foundations were laid. The ground floor was elevated above the surrounding grounds; beneath it, a large cistern was built to collect rain water flowing from the roof of the building.

As each story was completed, friends and relatives from Makkah and Taif were invited to attend a banquet to celebrate the accomplishment. At such affairs, the master builder would exalt the attributes of his structure and solicit the opinions of the guests. The party would end with the reading of Quranic verses as a thanksgiving to God for his blessings.

The wood used in this house was imported by sea from remote islands. The staircase was designed so that a mounted man could ride his steed to the upper floors. In fact, during his many stays in this house, it is said that King Abdulaziz al-Saud rode his horse up to his quarters.

This house stands in Jeddah to this day and has been designated as a historic landmark by the Saudi Department of Antiquities and Museums.

ARCHITECTURE

Left: *Qasr Shubra's southern facade and gardens. City of Taif.*
Above: *Qasr Shubra's main entrance.*
Right: *Qasr Shubra's wooden mushrabiyahs.*

The original Qasr Shubra, named after a similar Cairo palace, was a two-story structure built around 1858 by Abdallah bin Muhammad bin Aun, the Emir (Governor) of Makkah.

The present four-story building was erected in the early 1900s by Abdallah's son Ali, after he in turn became Emir of Makkah. While the stones used in the foundations and walls were excavated from nearby quarries, the marble for the formal entrance stairs (known as al-Samlek) was imported from Italy by sea to Jeddah, and carried up the mountains on camels to Taif. The wood for the mushrabyahs and interiors was brought in from Turkey, along with specialized craftsmen.

The palace was used by King Abdulaziz, when the government moved to Taif during the torrid summer months, and was later successively occupied by King Faisal and Prince Sultan bin Abdulaziz. In 1985, King Fahd designated the well-maintained palace as a Museum of Arab and Muslim Traditions.

Below: *Qasr Al-Muwaih.*
Al-Muwaih, 120 miles east of the city of Taif.
  Built by the Ottomans, the palace was expanded during the reign of King Abdulaziz.
Left: *Mosque dome detail, Qasr al-Muwaih.*
Right: *King Abdulaziz's outdoor audience court (* majlis*), Qasr al-Muwaih.*
Below right: *The mosque, Qasr al-Muwaih.*

ARCHITECTURE

219

Architecture

Left: *Castle with twin towers.*
Village of al-Malad, near the town of al-Baha, 120 miles south of the city of Taif.
Right: *Circular watchtower* (qasabah).
Town of Ahad Rufaidah, southeast of the city of Abha.
Below: *Square watch tower* (hosn), *built around 1850.*
Town of Muhail, 30 miles northwest of the city of Abha.

Below: *Interior court of the house of Salem bin Ali al-Majhud. Town of Bil-Jurshi, 160 miles south of the city of Taif.*
Right: *Built-in exterior stairs to the roof, house of al-Majhud.*

ARCHITECTURE

Above: *Carved wooden main door, house of al-Majhud.*
Left: *Ornate wooden pillar supporting the roof structure, house of al-Majhud.*

The Heritage of The Kingdom of Saudi Arabia

ARCHITECTURE

Far left: Five-story dwelling facade decorated with quartz pebbles (maru).
Town of Rujal Alma, an old caravan stop between the Red Sea and the Asir highlands, west of the city of Abha.
Left: Hand-decorated majlis *walls.*
Town of Rujal Alma.

   In this region, painted designs such as these graced many house walls and stairwells; the designs were created largely by women, many of whom were known in their communities for their skill and artistry. Dyes produced from local plants provided many colors of paint; the natural green, extracted mainly from the clover plant, was favored most.
Below: Windows decorated with quartz pebbles.
Village of Bani Mazen, west of the city of Abha.
Below left: Decorative hand-formed mud floor.
Town of Rujal Alma.
Following overleaf: Neighboring castles of al-Qaah and al-Muness, south of the city of Dhahran al-Janub.

225

The Heritage of The Kingdom of Saudi Arabia

Left: *Roof details with built-in ladder to the top. Village of al-Talha, east of the city of Dhahran al-Janub.*
Below: *Traditional dwellings extending over a village street. Village of al-Masqi, southeast of the city of Abha.*
Right: *Mud walls with hand-cut pieces of slate. Village of al-Ajamah, south of the town of Sarat Abaidah.*
   In this area, hand-cut pieces of slate, called rakaf, were laid in parallel courses to protect the face of the walls from the heavy rain and hail that characterize the region.

Below: *White-washed dwellings.*
Town of Sarat Abaidah, southeast of the city of Abha.
Right: *Grain tower, approximately 90 feet high, built around 1790.*
Village of al-Halaf, town of Sarat Abaidah.

Architecture

Left: *Reed dwelling (*ushah*).*
Village of al-Malha, north of the city of Jizan.
Right: *Partially constructed reed dwelling.*
Village of Abu al-Qaaed, north of the city of Jizan.
Below right: *Partially finished roof hut.*
Town of Sabya, north of the city of Jizan.
Below: *Hand-decorated plaster hut ceiling.*
Town of Sabya.

Left: *Al-Najdi Mosque, built in 1928 by Ibrahim al-Najdi al-Tamimi.*
Farasan Island, west of the city of Jizan.
Right: *Mihrab niche and built-in minbar balcony, al-Najdi Mosque.*
Below right: *Interior of al-Najdi Mosque.*

The mosque was built by a renowned pearl trader prior to the decline of the natural pearling industry. The walls are primarily composed of roughly cut hard coral blocks covered with gypsum. In addition to their decorative value, the carved gypsum screens filter the harsh sunlight and promote air circulation.

Left: *Facade of the al-Rifai house, a family of renowned pearl traders.*
Farasan Island.
Below: *Majlis of the house of Ali Muhammad Ahmad el-Rifai, adorned with carved gypsum walls, stained glass windows, and hand-painted wood ceiling beams.*

THE HERITAGE OF THE KINGDOM OF SAUDI ARABIA

Above: *Dwellings amidst terraced mountain slopes. Jabal Faifa, 50 miles northeast of the city of Jizan.*
Right: *Villages overlooking Wadi Qiyar. Jabal Quhbah, east of the city of Jizan.*
Following overleaf: *Castle (hosn) on the slopes of Jabal Faifa. Northeast of the city of Jizan.*

ARCHITECTURE

ARCHITECTURE

Preceding overleaf: *Twin watchtowers on top of boulder, home of Ali al-Radahi al-Harisi.*
Village of al-Qullah, Jabal al-Hashar, northeast of the city of Jizan.
Left: *Restored Governorate Castle* (Qasr al-Amarah) *main gate, built during the reign of King Abdulaziz.*
City of Najran.
Above: *Facade detail,* Qasr al-Amarah.
  Gypsum is used to highlight buildings as well as to protect the sun-dried mud construction from rapid erosion.
Opposite: *Al-Jaber seven-story castle.*
Village of Sagher, city of Najran.

Left: *Mud wall construction.*
Najran.
 Mud walls can be built without forming and pre-drying the mud (libin) in the sun. In this case, the walls are built in tapered horizontal rows that are slightly elevated at the corner, in order to increase their stability. Upon completion of each small portion, the builders smooth the side surfaces with a wood or metal tool. The walls are usually very thick to assure their structural strength.

Above: *Decorated rooftop of the castle of Shaikh Saleh bin Mane, Shaikh of the Abdallah tribes.*
Village of al-Hadan, city of Najran.
Right: *Al-Jaber family castles.*
City of Najran.
Following overleaf: *Decorated seven-story rooftop of the castle of Muhammad Saleh al-Zajur al-Sukur.*
Village of al-Dahda, city of Najran.

ARCHITECTURE

MARKETS AND CRAFTS

Left: *Traditional weaving made of dyed sheep's wool. Such hand-loomed pieces decorated the interior of bedouin tents.*
Following overleaf: *Girls wearing traditional jewelry and dressed up for a family celebration.*
Farasan Island, west of the city of Jizan.

MARKETS AND CRAFTS

TRADE AND THE ARABIAN PENINSULA

The Arabian Peninsula enjoyed a pivotal location on the trade routes of ancient nations. Goods and merchandise from these nations passed through the Peninsula since ancient times. In competing for influence and regional supremacy, all the neighboring powers that arose maintained commercial and political ties with the northern and southern parts of Arabia. They also crossed the Peninsula to secure the riches of southwestern Arabia, eastern Africa, India, and China.

The inhabitants of the Peninsula, whose towns lay on trade routes, benefited immensely from trading activities. In addition, some of the bedouins worked on caravans as guides or were retained for their fighting skills to escort the merchants and their convoys in safety.

ANCIENT ARABIAN STATES

Sailors long considered the Arabian Red Sea coast to be extremely dangerous because of offshore islands and reefs. Goods coming from the east were unloaded on the southern coast of Arabia prior to being transported overland to the Mediterranean. As a result, the ancient Arabian states that emerged in the southern parts and extended their presence to the north and other regions of Arabia were important centers on the trade routes to the Orient. Most notable among them was the Minean dynasty in Yemen around 1500 B.C., whose caravans traveled between the north and south along a land route parallel to the Red Sea and, to a lesser extent, along the eastern route that passed through Oman and the Arabian Gulf coast. At the time, the Mineans were the most powerful and affluent among Arab tribes, and constructed buildings, fortified cities, and dams. They were followed by the Himayrites (approximately 115 B.C.-525 A.D.), who lived in the southwestern parts of Arabia. They succeeded in controlling the major trade routes in the Peninsula. The Himayrites also subdued some of the Hijazi tribes and retained them to accompany and guard their trade caravans. During that same period, the state of Kinda rose in a remote part of the Arabian desert. Until its fall, around the fifth century A.D., Kinda had developed into a society whose civilized life was equaled only by its economic and political power.

In the northern part of the Peninsula, the Nabateans controlled the upper region of the Hijaz mountain chain between the sixth century B.C. and the second century A.D. Petra became their capital around 300 B.C. and remained a thriving trading center for centuries. Along with Petra, the city of Madain Saleh controlled the caravan routes that linked the Arabian Gulf, the Indian Ocean, and the Red Sea with the markets of the Mediterranean.

The fall of the Nabatean state in 106 A.D. was accompanied by the emergence of Palmyra, in the Syrian desert, as the most important trading post in the area. During the rule of the Roman emperor

Hadrian (117-138), the city-state prospered economically after it paid allegiance to the Roman Empire. Palmyra was situated at the crossroads of trade routes that connected India, China, and Persia in the east, Rome in the west, and Constantinople in the north. It also maintained trade relations with southern and western Arabia.

Feeling threatened by the growing independence and military strength of Palmyra, Emperor Aurelian of Rome invaded the city-state in 272, destroyed it, and captured its queen, thus ending the position of Palmyra as a successful Arabian trading center.

The Commercial Importance of Makkah and Madinah

The development of commerce among distant markets eventually led to the emergence of trade stations where caravans stopped for rest, provisions, and the exchange of goods. Even before the advent of Islam, Makkah and Madinah (then called Yathrib) were among the most famous of these stations. With time, the two cities developed into principal commercial centers in their own right, and their inhabitants began to compete with other centers in travel and trade.

Traditional bedouin jewelry, old souk of Riyadh.

By the beginning of the sixth century A.D., the tribe of Quraysh in Makkah had wrested control over trading activities from the Yemenis. The Qurayshis soon expanded their economic control over the Hijaz and other regions in the Peninsula. The wars that broke out between the Persians and the Byzantines ensured the ascendancy of Makkah and Madinah to positions of dominance.

The Hijazis, of course, had been involved in trade before the advent of Islam. Some made their fortunes trading with cities in Greater Syria, including Ailah, Gaza, Bursa, Damascus, Palmyra, and Aleppo. Their trade relations also extended to Egypt, Iraq, Abyssinia, and Yemen.

As an ancient holy place and an important location on the caravan route along the western coast of Arabia, Makkah became the largest trade station in the Peninsula. Around the year 440, a lord of the Quraysh tribe, Qussai bin Kilab, succeeded in regulating the affairs of his clan after years of infighting and divisiveness. He brought together the tribal shaikhs and elders, oversaw their activities and business dealings, and consulted them on all issues of importance to the city, including relations with its neighbors. The new sense of unity made Quraysh a very powerful tribe and an advanced commercial society with a strong economic structure. One of the outcomes of this reorganization in Makkah was what became known in the Arabian tradition as the Winter and Summer Journeys. In their quest for ever expanding markets, the Winter Journey (*rihlat al-shita*) carried Quraysh merchants to Yemen and Abyssinia, while the Summer Journey (*rihlat al-saif*) took them to Syria and Egypt. Capitalizing on Quraysh's new strength, the reach of the biannual expeditions was further enhanced as a result of trade pacts signed with neighboring nations.

Seasonal Markets

In addition to the permanent or occasional trade centers that developed in the Arabian Peninsula, some seasonal markets gained recognition as major fairs. The most notable were near Makkah and included Okaz, Majannah, and Dhu al-Majaz. The growth of these markets depended on the availability of products and crops according to regional and seasonal factors.

Each region was known for its particular riches. For example, incense, resin, myrrh, and dyes came from southern Arabia, especially Dhofar. Yemen was noted for swords, spears, and articles of clothing. Leather tanning and related crafts were the specialty of Taif. Bahrain produced an abundance of dates, and various parts of Syria traded in grains, cotton, oil, fine fabrics, and metal crafts. In the larger seasonal markets, tribes were assigned specific locations and could be recognized by their identifying banners.

One of the most famous seasonal fairs in Arabia

before Islam was known as the market, or *souk*, of Okaz. Each year, this market opened at the beginning of the month of *Dhu al-Qidah* (the eleventh month of the Arab lunar calendar) and lasted for two weeks. There were various and conflicting theories regarding the location of Souk Okaz until the Saudi Arabian historian, Muhammad bin Abdallah al-Blahad, resolved the issue by identifying its correct location as the meeting point of the Shirb and al-Ukhaidar valleys near Taif.

At the end of Souk Okaz, people moved to another market near Makkah called Souk Majannah, which also lasted two weeks. At the beginning of the following month, *Dhu al-Hijjah*, people proceeded to Souk al-Majaz near Arafah. This third market stayed open for eight days, when the Hajj season began in Makkah.

Souk Okaz survived for more than two centuries—from approximately 542 to 746. People from all over the Arabian Peninsula visited this vast public market. It was a place where traders, mostly from Arab lands, met and exchanged their merchandise.

Okaz was more than a prosperous hub of commercial activity. It was also an important center where tribal rules and regulations were decreed, disputes settled, judgements passed, and pacts and agreements signed or nullified. According to tradition, treaties and truces did not become effective until they were announced in Okaz. The souk also provided a forum for tribal races and competitions, as well as for religious preaching and missionary activities. Indeed, wise men, philosophers, priests, and monks made frequent visits to Okaz.

Okaz was particularly renowned as a forum for poetry readings and verse duels between competing poets. It played a crucial role in upgrading the linguistic skills of the tribes, unifying Arabic grammar and syntax, and establishing generally accepted modes of expression in poetry and oral discourse.

Souk Okaz came to an end in 746, when it was invaded, looted, and destroyed by the Kharijites. It never completely regained its past status and prominence.

In addition to the large, seasonal fairs, the towns and villages of Arabia established public markets in specific locations and on particular days of the week (hence the name "weekly markets"). They were generally erected in the main square, or market square, of a given community. The weekly markets usually opened from early morning until noon, with some lasting until sunset.

Market day was traditionally named after the day on which it took place—for example, the Wednesday Market (*souk al-Rubu*), the Thursday Market (*souk al-Khamis*), and so on. Merchants, farmers, craftsmen, and others throughout the immediate vicinity of the market regularly brought in their merchandise and used the opportunity to meet with people from other areas to conduct business and exchange information.

Potter at the weekly market of Najran. ca. 1965.

The weekly market also was significant because it fell on the day that court trials and hearings were publicly convened, rulings announced, and government decrees proclaimed. In addition, disputes were settled and conciliations were arranged on market day. It is no wonder, therefore, that tribes were very protective of their markets and keen on the orderly and peaceful conduct of activities there.

Weekly markets offered a variety of products, such as foodstuffs, clothing, and tools, needed by the inhabitants of towns and desert areas alike. Markets contained designated places for craftsmen to sell wooden products, construction materials, kitchen utensils, pottery (such as dishes, bowls, and pots), straw items (such as baskets, hats, mats, ropes, and sacks), various types of metal products, and crafts.

Markets were sectioned according to the class of product being sold. For instance, there were specific stands for perfumes, spices, and fabrics; some for coal, firewood, and fodder; and others for livestock. Some merchandise was exhibited in permanent stands erected in rows of similar design and usually protected by a covered portico. Grains, such as wheat, barley, corn, millet, and coffee, were displayed in large sacks or open straw baskets; they were measured by a special implement called a *saa*, made of wood or metal. Most merchandise, however, was exhibited in open, roofless markets. Makeshift stalls were constructed of tree trunks and covered with branches or with canvas; in their shade, parallel rows of goods were arranged.

Erected in specific quarters, food stands could be spotted easily by the smoke that billowed up from cooking pits and by the smell of grilled meat. One corner of the market was designated for the loading and unloading of supplies and goods carried by camels, mules, and other beasts of burden. Markets also had their peculiar noises and sounds—sellers auctioning off their wares in various phrases and accents, craftsmen hammering and forging their sundry products. At the end of the day, traders packed their belongings and returned home, leaving a place that would remain quiet and deserted until the market opened again on the same day of the following week.

CRAFTS

The Arabian Peninsula can be divided into two large geological regions: the Arabian Shelve and the Arabian Shield. The Arabian Shelve, which includes most of the Peninsula, slopes gently from the Arabian Gulf toward the western highlands. The Shelve is characterized by sedimentary rock, and holds the vast petroleum reserves that were discovered after King Abdulaziz authorized, in 1930, the prospection of the Kingdom's natural resources.

The Arabian Shield, which includes the western third of the Peninsula, is known for its igneous and metamorphic rocks where the ores of a variety of metals—especially gold, silver, copper, and iron—can be found. In fact, several Greek geographers mentioned the presence of mines in the Arabian Peninsula, and particularly of gold so pure that it needed no processing.

MINES

In 1926, an archaeological expedition from the American School for Oriental Research in Jerusalem unearthed a site near the northern end of the Gulf of Aqabah called Asyun Jaber and discovered several copper mines there. It also located a site where copper was smelted and purified in the Arrabah Valley in Palestine. Based on the pottery found in the area, it is estimated that the site dates back to the end of the third millennium B.C.

Ancient gold mines were later discovered in Mahd al-Dhahab, the "Cradle of Gold," north of Madinah. Mining activities at this site resumed early in this century but were later stopped. In 1982, King Fahd bin Abdulaziz inaugurated the resumption of operations at Mahd al-Dhahab.

Tools used in ancient times to extract gold were also excavated at several locations. These included millstones and grinding and crushing instruments such as pestles. In addition to copper and gold, zinc and lead ores were also found at sites in Najran and al-Quwaiyah, among others.

It is now believed that the early inhabitants of the Arabian Peninsula developed methods for extracting and smelting metals. In fact, the remains of some ancient furnaces stand to this day. Smelting was performed in towns and villages close to the mines. For example, in Mount Tahlal, near Abha, iron was smelted in furnaces that appear to have been used as recently as a few generations ago. The smelted metal was then moved in various forms and sizes and sold to craftsmen in nearby markets.

METALS

Craftsmen of various cities and towns resided and kept their shops in souks. Many of the smaller towns and villages had at least one blacksmith and one carpenter; other craftsmen traveled on their mounts to perform jobs on demand.

The city souks were sectioned according to the various crafts. For example, the blacksmiths' market was where kitchen utensils and agricultural tools were manufactured, and the arms market was where swords, daggers, arrows, and shields were made. The latter items were usually decorated, inlaid with gold and silver, and inscribed with the names of the makers and the owners. Handicrafts and tools were displayed on the entrance walls of the shops, thus signaling the shopkeepers' trades and attracting prospective buyers.

Brass was forged, molded, and decorated in the brass market. Most kitchen utensils, such as plates, pots, spoons, ladles, cups, water jugs, and dispensers of rosewater and orange blossom water, were made of brass and coated with tin, as were the various implements for making coffee.

Coffee has always occupied an important role in traditional Arabian hospitality. Its preparation and serving, almost a ritual, requires a set of utensils that include a large steel spoon with a long handle, a *mihmas*, that is used for roasting coffee beans over an open fire. The roasted beans are then ground in a *mihbash*, a large wooden mortar and pestle, or in a *hawan*, a smaller vessel usually made of copper. The grounded beans are brewed in three types of coffee pots: the largest one, called a *mitbakhah*, is used for boiling coffee. The medium-sized pot, the *misfat*, serves as an intermediate pot in which the coffee grounds are allowed to set, before pouring the coffee into the third and smallest pot. In the smallest pot, the *bahharah*, the coffee is aromatized with various condiments, such as allspice, cardamom, and carnation cloves.

Bronze, the result of mixing ninety percent copper and ten percent tin, was known since the end of the third century B.C. This alloy is most suitable for engraving because of its hardness, a characteristic lacking in pure copper.

Bronze manufacturing had become a well-established industry by the time Islam emerged in the Arabian Peninsula. It continued to be produced on a large scale during successive eras. High quality receptacles and utensils were made of bronze, and lesser quality items of iron or steel.

Bronze items engraved and inlaid with gold, silver, brass, and copper were crafted in the northern part of the Peninsula since the Sassanid period (225-650). The process of inlaying starts with chiseling designs on the metal and then filling the engraved area with another metal, usually of a different color and a higher quality. Muslim craftsmen in Makkah, Madinah, Oman, Sanaa, and many other Arabian cities created beautiful masterpieces of inlaid metal objects, including arms, jewelry, and kitchen utensils.

Through the ages, craftsmen who worked with gold and silver developed various methods for smelting gold and silver and mixing them with other metals to produce alloys appropriate for various applications— such as pulverization, engraving, inlaying, and plating.

The Arabian Peninsula was also famous for gold and silver handicrafts. Smiths fashioned and welded pieces of various geometric shapes together by blowing flames over the joints through hard metal pipes. Usually, their tools were named according to the type of metalwork they embodied, such as *arid* (wide), *mubassat* (flattened), *malfuf* (rolled), *mahfur* (engraved), and *manqush* (inscribed). As craftsmen of the Arabian Peninsula were exposed to the jewelry styles of Egypt, Syria, and Persia, traditional bedouin silver jewelry began to incorporate new features and similarities.

While jewelry is perceived as one of the oldest forms of Arabian decorative art, it is also considered as a traditional status symbol and a form of currency. To this day, rare pieces will appear in the jewelry souks after the annual pilgrimage. As a negotiable asset, jewelry is still regarded as insurance against hard times.

Pearls and Precious Stones

Makkah and Madinah were known for metalwork inlaid with precious stones, such as carnelian and turquoise, and shaped into bracelets and necklaces. The two cities also had a reputation for decorating cloth with pearls, which were abundant on the coasts of the Peninsula.

For a very long time, pearling played a significant role in the Arabian Gulf's economy. It is said that the port of Jubail alone harbored more than two hundred pearling boats at one time. In the shores of the Red Sea, the southwestern islands of Farasan also prospered from the trade. Until the world-wide recession of natural pearling in the late 1930s, diving for pearls was a very lucrative profession; divers learned it at an early age and passed the skill from generation to generation.

Since early times, the inhabitants of the coastal areas of the Arabian Peninsula also perfected the art of diving for and extracting corals from shallow waters. They possessed unmatched expertise in differentiating among the many types and colors of coral, which vary from white to light red to deep red to black; black coral is known by the name *yusr*. Arabian craftsmen excelled in inlaying coral with silver and gold.

Carnelian and turquoise were imported from the northern parts of the Arabian Peninsula, especially Sinai. Large quantities of these semi-precious stones also were imported from India and China. Craftsmen in Makkah and Madinah, who bought, polished, and cut the stones into various shapes and designs, were experts in determining the type of stone, its authenticity, and its degree of purity. The two cities also imported large quantities of diamonds, lapis lazuli, and other precious stones from India, China, and Afghanistan.

TEXTILES, LEATHER, AND FUR

Ordinary clothes were and still are made of cotton, which has been cultivated in some parts of the Arabian Peninsula since the early ages. One of the main characteristics of Arab garb are the long, wide, and floppy sleeves known as *ardan*. These and other clothing designs made their way outside the Arabian Peninsula as the Muslims conquered new lands.

Leather tanning was a popular craft in the Arabian Peninsula, especially among bedouins. Tanners

Traditional Najdi dress usually worn for special celebrations.

extracted dyes from leaves of various plants and trees, including pomegranate peels and gallnuts, for the dyeing process. Leather was used to make clothing, water skins, saddles, saddlebags, and footwear. Leather clothes were considered a sign of wealth and prosperity.

High-quality furs for winter wear were made of wool and sheepskin. These were tanned, dyed, processed in special ways, and decorated with colored cotton or silk material; furs also were embroidered with gold and silver threads.

For women, the most characteristically Arabian piece of clothing is called the *abayah*, a cloak-like, woolen wrap usually donned, in public, over a woman's garment. To this day, most *abayahs* are made of sheep's wool or camel hair and come in different colors, including white, black, and brown. Because of the stark look of the *abayah*, the rich diversity of women's garments was not usually visible in public. As a matter of fact, traditional women's wear within the Kingdom varies according to five regional styles that include the eastern shores, the northern plateaux, Najd, northern Hijaz, and Asir. A rich array of styles also exists in each region. Within this diversity, a common characteristic can be found in the fact that all garments were conceived as full length multi-layered outfits, designed to conserve the body's moisture. Additionally, the seams and edges of most traditional garments were sewn and decorated with cotton or silk threads, and sometimes with gold and silk embroidery. The intricacies and richness of the patterns varied according to each style.

In contrast to the colorful richness of traditional women's garments, men's clothing was, and has remained, rather simple. To this day, men wear a headcloth, called *ghutrah*, made of cotton or silk whose seams are embroidered with cotton threads. The *ghutrah* is worn over an embroidered cotton cap, called *kufiyyah* or *taqiyyah*, and fixed in place by an *iqal*, or headband, made of black wool or cotton fibers. In earlier times the headcloth was simply twisted and secured like a turban.

While the well-known white cotton robe, called *thawb*, appears to have been part of a long established tradition, it is only a contemporary interpretation of the men's traditional body-shirt. As a matter of fact, in some of the northern parts of the Kingdom as well as in the highlands, men are known to don darker and heavier wool *thawbs* during cold spells.

The traditional men's wardrobe included long pants, called *sirwall*, that were worn under an off-white cotton body-shirt similar to today's more tailored *thawb*. To complete the attire, a cotton jacket and an outer mantle, called *mishlah* or *abayah*, were worn on top. The outer mantle served to preserve body moisture during the day, and as a warming cover at night. In the highlands and in the northern deserts, where the climate can be bitter cold during the winter, men wore hand-woven wool *abayahs* lined with sheep fur. To this day, and on special occasions, men will also wear much lighter *abayahs* made of finely woven camel hair cloth, wool, or cotton. While remaining simple in style, the collars of these *abayahs* are usually embroidered with silk, silver, and gold threads.

It is important to note that hand-weaving, embroidery, and leather work were never limited to one gender. Men and women made many leather goods themselves, including handbags, saddlebags, and water skins. They also wove and embroidered clothing, as well as fabrics for tents, camel litters, saddle clothes, and colorful bedouin carpets.

POTTERY

Archaeological discoveries indicate that many areas of the Arabian Peninsula were known for making, coloring, and glazing all kinds of pottery. Clay pots and plates were used for cooking and preserving food and water. They were produced in an assortment of shapes and forms and generally followed ancient methods of pottery-making—with some variations and adjustments as new needs emerged.

While recent pottery appears to have lost some of its ancient artistic merits, it has remained a useful craft that combines form and function. In addition to clay utensils, craftsmen still excel in the fabrication of beautiful narrow-necked storage and water urns.

WOOD

Although the main Saudi Arabian mountain chains extend from the Yemeni borders in the south to Jordan in the north, they have not been a reliable source of timber over the centuries. While the oases palms were used in the construction of roofs, the trees were always more valued for their fruit. Tamarisk, by contrast, has been used as a main source of local wood. Over the centuries, most of the wood used in construction and crafts was imported from Africa and India. The wood was utilized in the manufacture of agricultural tools, such as sickles, axes, and shovels; it was also used in construction to make doors and windows. While its function was more limited when it came to the fabrication of weaponry, wood was nevertheless needed to make dagger and sword handles, scabbards, and powder rifles. The latter items were engraved according to regional styles.

Handicrafts produced at the carpenters' markets included wooden chests, bowls and saddle frames, as well as the valuable well pulleys. The chests, wooden bowls and saddle frames were usually studded with decorative brass or silver nails. Doors, windows, and window sills were made of different types of wood and designed with local preferences in mind. In Najd, for example, they were created with tamarisk wood and palm branches, adorned with carved geometric designs, painted with different colors, and decorated with large nails. In the Hijaz and Asir, doors and windows were made of wild olive and other kinds of wood adorned with carved decorations, and painted with a preservative material extracted from tar.

Produced in the Tihamah region, tar is a gummiferous substance that was extracted from trees, such as the wild olive and the tamarisk. Branches of these trees were cut into small pieces, stacked in closed metal or clay containers each with an opening in its base, and heated until the thick, black liquid flowed into a gathering hole in the ground. Tar also was used in the Arabian Peninsula to treat certain animal skin diseases inflicted by insect bites.

Doors of houses were locked by one or more latches or bolts made of wood and fitted with a wooden lock (*dabbah*); the key was made of wood, metal, or a combination of both. The tamarisk or wild olive wood lock had two parts: the upper called *al-majra* (the path) and the lower, *al-sikrah* (the latch). Lock-making was the speciality of certain craftsmen, who handed their knowledge down through the generations. Indeed, many old building doors in Makkah, Madinah, Riyadh, Jeddah, and Taif, as well as the wood decorations on some of the remaining facades, stand as witnesses to the skill, talent, and aesthetic sense of the craftsmen who made them.

One of the handicrafts that required special skill was the manufacture of large wooden trays. The region of Asir was known for competent craftsmen who produced the best of these trays. Some of the larger trays measured up to three feet in diameter and were very expensive. They were used to serve food at large banquets and festive events.

Ships were built around the Arabian coasts for centuries. Shipbuilders even constructed dhows that crossed the high seas and oceans, reaching India, China, and Far Eastern islands, as well as East African and Mediterranean coasts. Ship owners, sailors, and crew members, all inhabitants of the Arabian Peninsula and its surrounding areas, were experts in sailing, navigation, and oceanography. They studied winds and sea currents and their seasons; they also had extensive knowledge of the design and the inner workings of ships and sails.

Arab seamen began their adventures across the seas by making short trips along the Arabian coast. At first, their small boats were made of stems and branches of palm or other trees, tied together by special ropes, and made watertight with tar. With time, the industry developed and larger vessels, capable of sustaining the long trips east, were built. To this day, traditional shipbuilding remains a thriving craft in several of the Kingdom's coastal towns.

MARKETS AND CRAFTS

Left: *Bedouin leather shoes (*zarabil*) with a knitted cotton upper section, from the early 1900s.*
Below: *Called* hawdaj, *this wood and wool cabin, fastened on a camel's back, allowed women to travel in relative comfort.*
Below left: *Hand-loomed tent interior curtain, called* riwaq, *used to separate one tent section from another.*

Opposite: *Bedouin women's handbag, made of leather and overlaid with silver gilding.*
Following page: *Ancient mine shaft entrance with steps carved in the rock.*
Riqayyan, 120 miles west of the city of Riyadh.

The Heritage of The Kingdom of Saudi Arabia

Markets and Crafts

THE HERITAGE OF THE KINGDOM OF SAUDI ARABIA

MARKETS AND CRAFTS

Preceding page: *Craftsman making a traditional copper pot.*
Old market, city of Riyadh.
Left: *Coppersmith coating the inside of a brass coffeepot with tin. Unless coated, brass copper utensils cannot be used for cooking.*
Old souk, city of Riyadh.
Above: *Brass coffeepot* (dallah), *representative of the Makkah style and dating to approximately 1930.*
Old souk, city of Makkah.
Above right: *Brass mortars and pestles used for grinding spices. Crafted in the early 1900s, the smaller is believed to have been made in Makkah, and the larger in al-Hasa.*
Old souk, city of Makkah
Following page: *Gunsmith making a new gun handle. Old souk, city of Riyadh.*

The Heritage of The Kingdom of Saudi Arabia

Markets and Crafts

265

THE HERITAGE OF THE KINGDOM OF SAUDI ARABIA

Preceding page: *Silversmith blowing flames to fuse a piece of jewelry.*
Jewelry souk, city of Riyadh.
Right: *Frankincense burning in a* mabkhara, *a traditional wood container studded with brass.*
Old souk, city of Riyadh.
Below: *Incense vendor. Old souk, city of Riyadh.*
Opposite: *Tailor finishing the collar of an* abayah *with gold threads.*
Old souk, city of Riyadh.

In the highlands and in the northern deserts, where the climate can be bitter cold during the winter, men wear handwoven wool abayahs lined with sheep fur. On special occasions men also wear light abayahs, called mishlahs made of finely woven camel hair or silk threads.

Markets and Crafts

The Heritage of The Kingdom of Saudi Arabia

MARKETS AND CRAFTS

Left: *Sandal-maker working on a pair of leather* niaal.
Old leather souk, city of Riyadh.

  In the past, hand-weaving, embroidery, and leatherwork were not limited to clothing. Men and women made many leather goods themselves, including handbags, saddlebags, and waterskins.
Right: *A craftsman scales his work with a handmade wooden compass.*
Town of Unaizah, 300 miles northwest of the city of Riyadh.
Below: *Carving and decorating a set of wooden doors with a sharp knife, a craftsman follows the minute patterns of a traditional design.*
Town of Unaizah.

THE HERITAGE OF THE KINGDOM OF SAUDI ARABIA

Below: *Camel race starting line.*
City of Taif.
Right: *Approaching the finish line, two riders are cheered by the crowd.*
City of Taif.

Traditional camel races used to be held in conjunction with large seasonal fairs and markets, such as the historic Souk Okaz fair. To this date, the races have maintained a strong popular appeal.

Opposite: *Ruins of Souk Okaz. East of the city of Taif.*

Souk Okaz was for over two centuries one of the most famous seasonal fairs in Arabia. Prior to being invaded and looted by the Kharijites in 746 A.D., it was one of the most prosperous commercial hubs of the Arabian Peninsula. The souk also provided a forum for tribal races and competitions, and was particularly renowned for its poetry readings and verse duels between competing poets.

MARKETS AND CRAFTS

Right: *Dance of the* Mezmar.
Performed to the beat of five drums, with two dancers in the center, the dance is a dexterity game that involves skillful stick movements.
Left and below: *Traditional* Arda *dance.*
Considered one of the oldest forms of Arabian dance, the Arda *is a popular form of celebration in which people from all walks of life take part in a ceremonial procession. The dance has evolved since the days of King Abdulaziz and symbolizes the unity of the Kingdom. When performed at large gatherings, the* Arda *draws people from the audience. On special occasions, the King himself may join in, too*

273

THE HERITAGE OF THE KINGDOM OF SAUDI ARABIA

Left: *The Kaabah and the Makkah Grand Mosque's courtyard.*
Right: *Embroidered* Kiswah *panel adorning the Kaabah door. Grand Mosque of Makkah.*
Below: Kiswah *panel adorned with gold embroidered verses from the Quran.*

The Kiswah *is the great black cloth covering the Kaabah. The sacred stone cubic structure is considered the "House of God" and the physical center of Islam.*

The Kaabah has been honored for close to 4000 years, since the days of the Patriarch Abraham. From early Islamic times, the caliphs and other Muslim rulers considered it a privilege and a religious duty to provide the Kiswah. *Nowadays, the cloth is made in Makkah and each new* Kiswah *is adorned with verses from the Quran which are richly woven and embroidered in gold and silver. Covering the four sides of the Kaabah, each* Kiswah *measures approximately 28,500 square feet and is replaced annually.*

The Heritage of The Kingdom of Saudi Arabia

Below: Burga, *also called* khimar, *adorned with silver coins and other decorative pieces.*

While a variety of veil designs was in use throughout the Kingdom, this particular style was worn by women in Madinah in the early 1900s.

Right: *Gold jewelry store.*
City of Makkah.

Jewelry is considered one of the oldest forms of Arabian decorative art. It is also regarded as a traditional status symbol and a form of currency. As a negotiable asset, jewelry was long valued as insurance against hard times.

MARKETS AND CRAFTS

The Heritage of The Kingdom of Saudi Arabia

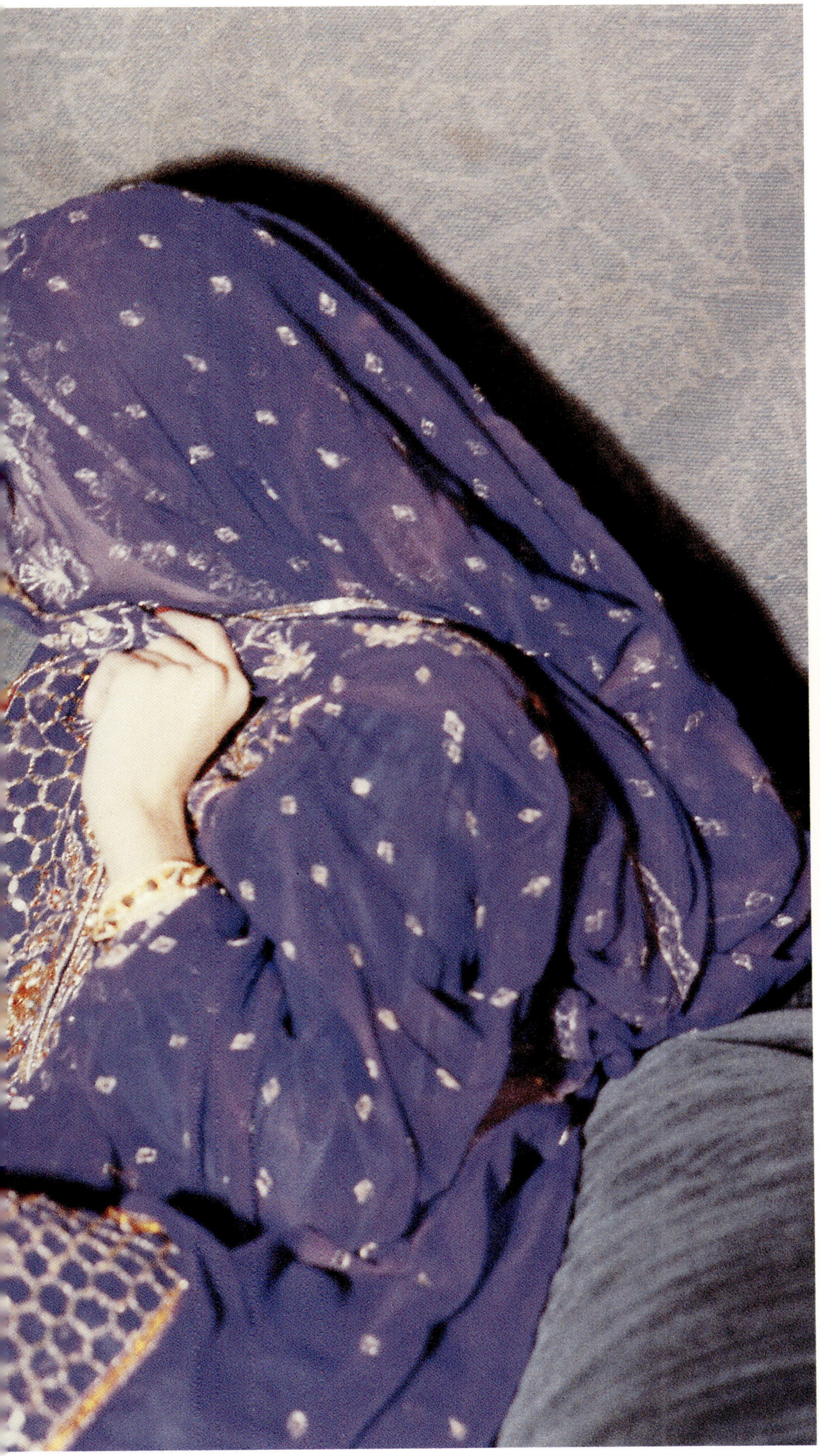

MARKETS AND CRAFTS

Left: *Festive silk chiffon ensembles with rich sequins and gold embroidery. These coordinated two-piece ensembles include a simple dress and an elaborate chiffon overdress. The outfits are similar to the ceremonial Najdi overdress called* muqassab. *They are still worn on special occasions, and their cut, colors, and embroidery are considered representative of the eastern region.*

Above: *Ceremonial dress incorporating the Kingdom's palm tree and cross swords emblem. The richly embroidered dress is about fifty years old and represents the evolution of previous traditional trends.*

Markets and Crafts

Left: *Swordsmith at the weekly market.*
Village of Harub, northeast of the city of Jizan.
Right and below: *Vendors of knives and steel tools.*
Village of Harub.
Following overleaf left: *Ornate dagger and scabbard with meticulous work and hand-embroidered silk belt.*
Town of Khamis Mushait, east of the city of Abha.
Following overleaf right: *Dagger adorned with silk threads and worn by a provincial guard (khawi).*
Town of al-Harajah, southeast of the city of Abha.

The sword (saif) and the dagger (janbiyah) were considered necessary for self-defense until the turmoil of the early 1900s. Now, swords are symbolically displayed during special ceremonial occasions, and daggers are popular in certain regions as an element of adornment for men.

Some of the dagger handles are made of wood, preferably ebony. Traditionally, the most prized handles are made of ibex or mountain goat's horn and adorned with silver. The scabbard usually is made of wood encased in leather or fabric and decorated with silverwork and precious stones.

The Heritage of The Kingdom of Saudi Arabia

MARKETS AND CRAFTS

THE HERITAGE OF THE KINGDOM OF SAUDI ARABIA

Right: *Vendor of straw hats, mats, and containers.*
Town of al-Harajah, southeast of the city of Abha.
Below: *Traditional straw hats and baskets at the weekly market.*
Village of Abu Arish, east of the city of Jizan.
   While straw hats are not worn in most areas of the Kingdom, they are part of the local culture of western Asir and Jizan. It is speculated that the hats date back to the Portuguese presence in the Peninsula, approximately 200 years ago.
Opposite: *Vendor of handmade stone cooking pots with cone-shaped straw lids.*
Old souk, city of Najran.

Markets and Crafts

Preceding overleaf: *Woodcarver using a lathe to carve a piece of wood.*
Old souk, city of Najran.
Right: *Carpenter making a* huddah, *a wooden structure covered with leather and fabric that serves as a camel saddle.*
City of Najran.
Below: *Wooden plate artisan.*
City of Najran.

Najran and the region of Asir were known for competent craftsmen who produced the best wooden plates. Some of the larger plates measured up to three feet in diameter and were used to serve food at large banquets and festive events.

Markets and Crafts

MARKETS AND CRAFTS

Left: *Display of the variety and artfulness of silver bedouin jewelry inlaid with precious stones.*
Town of Khamis Mushait, east of the city of Abha.
Above: *Goldsmith welding jewelry pieces.*
Town of Khamis Mushait.

The Heritage of The Kingdom of Saudi Arabia

Far left: *Necklace with amber beads separated by hollow silver filigree beads.*

Amber was always a prized ornament in bedouin jewelry and used to be collected on the shores of the Arabian sea. The ornate rectangular pendant is a charm, hirz, with little bells traditionally also considered charms.

Left: *Silver necklace pendant with amber beads, silver filigree balls, coins, small charm bells, and a cylindrical hirz.*

Below: *Silver necklace with rich ornate plates linked by eight delicate chains. The two triangular end pieces support little bells suspended from silver wires adorned with silver threads. The little heart shapes above the mounted coins are considered to be charms, and the four red stones probably replace the carnelian and coral that once highlighted the necklace.*

Below left: *Called* kirdan, *this style of neck piece is characterized by its meshed appearance. This* kirdan *includes five threaded rows of highly ornate silver plates, chain links, rings, and beads. The bottom row ends with two links of smaller silver beads. Kirdans usually vary in length; some may extend from the neckline to the waist.*

292

Markets and Crafts

Left: *Cylindrical sealed charm with intricate filigree work. The charm was probably part of a more important necklace.*
Below: *Necklace with amber beads separated by hollow silver filigree beads. The designs on the beads and the variations in their patina suggest that they were probably assembled from different silver ornaments.*
Right: *Pair of hollow silver bracelets, with surface-applied decorative diamond-shaped plates and granulated flower shapes and filigrees. The ends are welded together and secured with filigree diamond-shaped plates.*
Below right: *Hand-woven neckband with 30 individual and highly ornate chained pendants incorporating filigree work, silver beads, and coins. Emphasizing the character of the jewelry as a negotiable asset, bedouin jewelry frequently incorporates a variety of coins.*
Below left: *Decorated silver choker band, called kirdala, with elongated beads and little hollow balls. Some balls are linked to the choker or suspended from delicate silver chains.*

MARKETS AND CRAFTS

Left: *Shepherds bargaining at the livestock market. Al-Farshah, northeast of the city of Jizan.*
Below: *Shepherds at the weekly market. Town of al-Farshah.*
    The wearing of laurel and herb wreaths as a form of adornment is typical of this area.
Following overleaf: *Fruit and vegetable market. City of Abha.*

Below: *Potter working on a hand-operated wheel. City of Jizan.*
Right: *Traditional clay pots used for water storage. The narrow necks afford access and prevent evaporation. City of Jizan.*
Opposite: *Shaping and decorating clay on a potter's wheel. City of Jizan.*

The Heritage of The Kingdom of Saudi Arabia

302

MARKETS AND CRAFTS

Preceding overleaf: *Old jewelry chest containing pearls and the implements to measure and weigh them.*
Farasan Islands, southeast of the city of Jizan.
Opposite: *Pearl diver.*
Farasan Islands.
Left: *Pearl trader at his home.*
Farasan Islands.

For generations, diving for pearls remained a main source of income in the Arabian Gulf and along the southwestern shores of the Kingdom's Red Sea. A few still dive for pearls, but it is now largely a disappearing trade.
Below: *Shipyard.*
City of Jizan.

Dhows, used both as small trading vessels and as fishing boats, are still made in some of the coastal ports of the Kingdom.
Following overleaf: *Dhow at sunrise.*
Arabian Gulf.

BIBLIOGRAPHY

Non-Arabic Sources

Al-Ansari, Abdul Rahman
Studies in the History of Arabia, Vol. 1.
University of Riyadh, Riyadh, 1979.
Qaryat al-Fau
University of Riyadh, Riyadh, 1982.
Studies in the History of Arabia, Vol. 2.
University of Riyadh, Riyadh, 1984.

Alavi, Ziaudin
Arab Geography in the Ninth and Tenth Centuries.
Aligarh Muslim University, Aligarh, 1965.

Al-Rashid, Saad bin Abd al-Aziz
Al-Rabadhah
King Saud University, Riyadh, 1986.

Ashkenazi, T.
The Anazah Tribes.
Southwestern Journal of Anthropology, New Mexico, 1948.

Balsan, Francois
A travers l'Arabie inconnue...
Amiot-Dumont, Paris 1954.

Batrik, Abdel Hamid M.
Turkish and Egytian Rule in Arabia 1810-1814 (Ph.D. dissertation).
London University, London, 1947.

Blunt, Anne
A Pilgrimage to Nejd, the Cradle of the Arab Race.
John Murray, London, 1881.

Botta, Paul Emile
Notice sur un Voyage dans l'Arabie Heureuse.
Musee d'histoire naturelle, Paris, 1841.

Bouni, A.
Une nouvelle borne Militaire de Trajan dans la Palmyrène.
AAS, Tome X, 1960.

Brown, W.R.
The Horse of the Desert.
Macmillan, New York, 1948.

Buchan, James
Jeddah Old and New.
Stacey International, London, 1980.

Bullard, Reader
The Camels Must Go.
Faber and Faber, London, 1961.

Burton, Richard
Personal Narrative of a Pilgrimage to Al-Madinah and Meccah.
Longman, London, 1855.

Buttler, H.C.
Ancient Architecture in Syria.
Publication of Princeton University Archaeological Excavation, Section A, Part 4.
Leiden, 1914.

Büttiker, Prof. Wilhelm
The Wildlife of Saudi Arabia and its Neighbours.
Stacey International, London, 1981.

Canard, Marius
Byzance et les Musulmans du Proche Orient.
London, Variorum Reprints, 1973.

Creswell, K.A.C.
Early Muslim Architecture, Vol. 1 (in two parts).

Oxford, 2nd Ed., 1969.
A Short Account of Early Muslim Architecture.
Beirut, 1968.

Dickson, H.R.P.
The Arab of the Desert.
Hodder and Stoughton, London, 1957.

Didier, Charles
Séjour chez le Grand-Chérif de la Mekke.
Hachette, Paris, 1857.

Dostal, Walter
Ethnographic Atlas of Asir.
Oesterreichische Akademie der Wissenschaften, Vienna, 1983.

Doughty, Charles Montagu
Travels in Arabia Deserta, 2 vols.
Jonathan Cape, London, 1921.
Wanderings in Arabia.
Duckworth, London, 1939

Du Couret, Louis (called Abd al-Hamid Bey)
Life in the Desert.
Translated from the French, New York, 1860.

Fisher, Sydney N.
The Middle East: A History.
Knopf, New York, 1959.

Goldsmith, Richard
Mineral Resources of the Southern Hijaz Quadrangle.
Kingdom of Saudi Arabia, Mineral Resources Bulletin No. 5.
Jeddah, 1971.

Hazard, Harry W.
The Arabian Peninsula.
Doubleday, New York, 1964.

Hitti, Philip K.
History of the Arabs.
Macmillan, London and New York, 10th Ed., 1970.

Hogarth, D.G.
The Penetration of Arabia.
Stockes, New York, 1904.

Hopwood, Derek
The Arabian Peninsula.
Allen and Unwin, London, 1972.

Hourani, George Fadlo
Arab Seafaring.
Princeton University Press, Princeton, 1951.

Kennedy, A.B.W.
Petra—Its History and Monuments.
London, 1925.

Kiernan, Reginald H.
The Unveiling of Arabia; The Story of Arabian Travel and Discovery.
Harrap & Co. Ltd., London, 1937.

King, Geoffrey R.D.
The Historical Mosques of Saudi Arabia.
Longman, Harlow, 1986.

Lawrence, T.E.
Seven Pillars of Wisdom.
Cape, London, 1935.

Le Bon, Gustave
La Civilisation des Arabes.
Minerva, Geneva, 1974.

Le Strange, G.
Baghdad during the Abbasid Caliphate.
London, 1924.

Lippens, Philippe
Expédition en Arabie Centrale.
Adrien-Maisonneuve, Paris, 1956.

Mandel, Gabriele
Il Regno di Saba, Ultimo Paradiso Archaeologico.
Milano, Sugar, 1973.

McClure, Harold A.
The Arabian Peninsula and Prehistoric Populations.
Coconut Grove, Florida, 1971.

Miller, J.
The Spice Trade of the Roman Empire, 29 B.C.–641 A.D.
Oxford, 1969.

Musil, Alois
Arabia Petraea.
Hoelder, Vienna, 1907.
The Northern Hejaz.
American Geographical Society, New York, 1926.
Arabia Deserta.
American Geographical Society, New York, 1927.

Naval Intelligence Division
Admiralty Handbook of Arabia, 2 vols.
London, 1917.
Admiralty Handbook—Western Arabia and the Red Sea.
London, 1946.

Niebuhr, Karsten
Déscription de l'Arabie (trans. F.L. Mourier).
Moller, Copenhagen, 1776; revised Ed., 1779.

Palgrave, William G.
Narrative of a Year's Journey Through Central and Eastern Arabia (1862-63), 2 vols.
London, 1865, 1969.

Philby, H. St. John B.
The Heart of Arabia.
Constable, London, 1922.
The Empty Quarter.
Henry Holt, New York, 1933.
Arabian Days.
Robert Hale, London, 1948.
Arabian Highlands.

New York, Cornell University Press, 1952
Forty Years in the Wilderness.
Robert Hale, London, 1957.
Philby-Ryckmans-Lippens.
Expédition Philby-Ryckmans-Lippens en Arabie, 1951-1952.
Publications Universitaires, Louvain, 1962.
Poidebard, A.
La Trace de Rome dans le désert de Syrie (Text et Atlas).
Paris, 1934.
Ross, Heather Colyer
Bedouin Jewellery in Saudi Arabia.
Stacey International, London, 1978.
Salah, Said
Brief Pictorial Guide to Saudi Arabia.
Alkhobar, International Publication Agencies, 1971.
Sauvaget, J.E.
Relations de la Chine et de L'Inde.
Translated from the work of Hasan Ibn Yazid Abu Zaid Al-Sirafi.
Belles Lettres, Paris, 1948.
Strass, Sir Ronald
Orientations.
Ivor, Nicholson and Watson, London, 1939.

Syed, Ayub
India and the Arab World.
Orient Publishers, New Delhi, 1965.
Talib, Kaizer
Shelter in Saudi Arabia
Academy Editions, London, 1984.
Tamisier, Maurice
Voyages en Arabie.
Sejour dans le Hedjaz-Campagne d'Assir.
Paris, L.Desessart, 1840.
Thesiger, Wilfred
Arabian Sands.
Book Club Associates, London, 1959.
Thomas, Bertram
Arabia Felix; Across the "Empty Quarter" of Arabia.
Scribner's Sons, New York, 1932.
The Arabs.
Butterworth, London, 1937.
Van Beck, G.W.
Frankincense and Myrrh.
The Biblical Archaeologist, Vol. XXII, 1960.
Wellsted, J.R.
Travels in Arabia.
Murray, London, 1838.

Selected Arabic Sources

Al-Alussi, Mahmud Chuqri
Tarikh Najd.
Al-Matbaah al-Salfiyah, Cairo, 1928 (1347 A.H.).
Al-Aqili, Muhammad Ahmad
Tarikh al-Mikhlaf al-Sulaimani.
Matbaat al-Riyadh, Riyadh 1958 (1378 A.H.).
Al-Hamadani, Hassan bin Ahmad
Sifat Jazirat al-Arab.
Marqaz al-Dirassah, Sanaa, 1983 (1404 A.H.).
Al-Jasser, Hamad
Fi Sarat Ghamed wa Zahran.
Matbaat al-Mutanabi, Beirut, 1971 (1391 A.H.).
Al-Jaziri, Abdulkader bin Muhammad
Darar al-Fawaed al-Munazamah Fi Akhbar al-Hajj...
Al-Matbaah al-Salfiyah, Cairo, 1964 (1384 A.H.).
Al-Rihani, Amin
Muluk al-Arab.
Dar Amin al-Rihani, Beirut, 1960 (1380 A.H.).
Al-Shihabi, Mustapha al-Amir
Al-Jughrafiyun al-Arab.

Dar al-Maaref, Cairo, 1962 (1382 A.H.).
Al-Tabari, Abu Jufar Muhammad Jarir
Tarikh al-Muluk.
Dar al-Qamus al-Hadith, Beirut, 1958 (1388 A.H.).
Al-Zirqali, Khayr al-Din
Shubh al-Jazirah al-Arabiyah Fi Ahd al-Maleq Abdulaziz.
Matabe Dar al-Qalam, Beirut, 1970 (1390 A.H.).
Fakhri, Ahmad
Dirasat Fi Tarikh al-Sharq al-Qadim.
Maktabat al-Anglo al-Masriyah, Cairo, 1963 (1383 A.H.).
Hafez, Wahbeh
Jazirat al-Arab Fi al-Qarn al-Ishrin.
Lajnat al-Talif Wa al-Tarjamah, Cairo, 1967 (1387 A.H.).
Hamidah, Abdulrahman
Alam al-Jughrafiyin al-Arab.
Dar al-Fiqr, Damascus, 1969 (1389 A.H.).
Hamzah, Fuad
Qalb Jazirat al-Arab.

Maktabat al-Nasr al-Haditha, Riyadh, 2nd Ed., 1968 (1388 A.H.).
Fi Bilad Assir.
Maktabat al-Nasr al-Haditha, Riyadh, 2nd Ed., 1968 (1388 A.H.).

Hassan, Ibrahim Hassan
Tarikh al-Islam.
Maktabat al-Nahda al-Masriyah, Cairo, 1964 (1384 A.H.).

Hassan, Muhammad Zaki
Al-Rahalah al-Muslimun Fi Al-Qurun al-Wusta.
Dar al-Maaref, Cairo, 1945 (1365 A.H.).

Hussain, Fawzi
Al-Milaha al-Arabiyah Fi al-Qurun al-Wusta.
Muhadarat al-Mawsem al-Thaqafi, Kuwait, 1956 (1376 A.H.).

Ibn Absi, Ibrahim bin Saleh
Aqd al-Durar Fima Waqaa Fi Najd...
Maktabat al-Nahada, Riyadh, 1952 (1372 A.H.).

Ibn al-Athir (Ali bin Abi al-Maqarem al-Chibani)
Al-Kamel Fi al-Tarikh.
Al-Maktabah al-Azhariyah, Cairo, 1883 (1301 A.H.).

Ibn Blehed, Muhammad bin Abdallah
Sahih al-Akhbar Ama Fi Bilad al-Arab min Athaar.
Riyadh, 2nd Ed., 1972 (1392 A.H.).

Ibn Bushr, Othman bin Abdallah
Unwan al-Majd Fi Tarikh Najd.
Matbuat Dar al-Malek Abdulaziz, 1983 (1403 A.H.).

Ibn Eissa, Ibrahim bin Saleh
Akd al-Darar Fima Wakaa Fi Najd Mina al-Hawadess.
Maktabat al-Nahda, Riyadh, 1952 (1372 A.H.).

Ibn Iyass, Muhammad bin Ahmad
Badae al-Zuhur Fi Wakae al-Duhur.
Edited by Muhammad Mustapha.
Cairo, 1961 (1381 A.H.).

Ibn Khaldun, Abdulrahman bin Muhammad
Al-Muqadimah.
Lajnat al-Bayan al-Arabi, 1958 (1378 A.H.).

Ibn Majed, Chihabeldin Ahmad
Kitab al-Fawaed Fi Usul Ilm al-Bahr Wa al-Kawaed;
Edited by Ibrahim Khoury and Izat Hassan.
Damascus, 1971 (1391 A.H.).

Ibrahim bin Ishak bin Ibrahim (Abu al-Hassan al-Harbi)
Al-Manaseq Wa Turoq al-Hajj Wa Maalem al-Jazirah.
Edited by Hamad al-Jassir.
Dar al-Yamamah, Riyadh, 1969 (1389 A.H.).

Jawad, Ali
Al-Mufassal Fi Tarikh al-Arab Qabl al-Islam.
Dar al-Malayin. Beirut, 1973 (1393 A.H.).

Jumah, Ibrahim
Al-Atlas al-Tarikhi Lildawlah al-Saudiyah.
Matbuat Darat al-Malek Abdulaziz, 1979 (1399 A.H.).

Kahala, Omar Reda
Jughrafiyat Shubh Jazirat al-Arab.
Al-Matbaah al-Hashimiyah, Damascus, 1944 (1364